WHITE MEAT

JIM BRISBY &
SIMON WOODS

CRANSWICK

First published in Great Britain in 2017 by Cranswick PLC.
Text copyright © Jim Brisby & Simon Woods 2017
Design & layout copyright © Face Publications 2017
Photography copyright © Paul Robinson 2017

A CIP catalogue record of this book is available from the British Library.
ISBN 9781527207516

Produced in association with Face Publications
www.facepublications.com

Printed and bound in Italy

Written by Jim Brisby & Simon Woods
Art direction by Anthony Hodgson
Design by Joel Archer
Edited by Jeannie Swales
Photography by Paul Robinson
Additional words by Chandos Elletson

WHITE MEAT

FOREWORD

— Jim Brisby

Pork is the most consumed meat across the globe – which isn't surprising because, when you learn to cook it properly and get the best out of it, it offers the best of both worlds. You can be light and healthy with the lean cuts, or rich and tasty with the cuts that contain more fat. I grew up on a pig farm so I understand what effect the combination of higher animal welfare, good feed and the right breeds of pig have on producing quality pork.

The majority of people have only a tiny repertoire of pork recipes, which is a shame because, if you select the right cuts, pork is high in protein and low in fat. It's simple and quick to cook and brilliant paired with other flavours, which is one of the main reasons pork is so popular in every corner of the world.

We in the UK have had a love affair with pork for centuries: roast pork and crackling, gammon and pineapple, ham sandwiches, sausages and bacon rolls are all ingrained in the national psyche. And yet it's incredible how many people tell me they get frustrated by not being able to make proper crackling. The secret is simply a matter of knowing which cut to buy (without the fat you have no flavour), adding boiling water and using a very sharp knife – Simon Woods will explain all later in the book!

Chicken isn't far behind pork as one of the world's most popular meats, and in the UK it's our number one choice. Most of us cook or eat chicken regularly as it's uncomplicated and naturally healthy. However, by adopting a 'whole bird' mentality you can develop a whole new repertoire of recipes and ideas. The legs, drumsticks and wings are so tasty and, like pork, are brilliant with other flavours.

White Meat is a book about pork and poultry. It's full of ideas, recipes, flavours and techniques to help you get the best out of both meats. It was born from a desire to pass on the knowledge that we at Cranswick have accumulated over the years as a market leader in pork and poultry production. When we decided to turn our knowledge into a book and started to compile all our favourite foods and techniques, it was clear we had a mountain of material from across the world to choose from.

What's thrilling to me is that we're coming at the subject from a new direction. This is a book that looks at pork and chicken in a completely new light, using modern techniques and cooking methods from different cultures, but at the same time tapping into the classic dishes that everyone wants to master.

PART OF OUR
PHILOSOPHY HAS
ALWAYS BEEN TO
FIND ARTISAN FOOD
PRODUCERS AND
WORK WITH THEM
TO SUPPLY PREMIUM
FOOD TO AS MANY
PEOPLE AS WE CAN.

INTRODUCTION

12 — 21

Cranswick is a Yorkshire food company with a proud heritage. Over the last 40 years we've done everything from producing pig feed, to rearing livestock, and finally producing premium quality food.

Our business is built around how to get the best out of pork and poultry. This book shares our knowledge, expertise and recipes.

People's attitudes to food have changed dramatically. We eat out so often now that it's almost a daily ritual. We enjoy take-away food from every corner of the globe and travel so widely that world cuisines are ingrained in our subconscious.

Part of our company's philosophy is to find artisan food producers and work with them to supply premium food to as many people as possible. In the 1990s, for example, Martin Heap was running a successful small business producing a range of unique gourmet sausages from Smithfield Market. When we came across his shop, with its queue out of the door and down the street, we knew we'd found someone special who we could work with to develop food that would appeal to a much wider audience.

Today, twenty-something years later, we have a growing list of food heroes working with us who are experts in bacon, pastry, wood-smoked barbecue meats, cured meats and, of course, sausages, which has given us a unique understanding of consumer products.

Although consumers are generally time-poor and need help with convenience, there are also times when they want to produce great food from scratch. Our recipes reflect where we feel food is in 2017, whilst embracing traditions and our culinary history.

When we started writing the book we concentrated on the classics - with recipes including things like crackling, which a lot of home cooks want but struggle with. We soon realised that what we wanted to achieve was a book that offered help and advice on the quick, the simple and the healthy as well as the blow-out, the barbecue and the celebration. The recipes are broken down into three chapters: Modern Classics, Small Plates and Street Food.

This cookbook shares our passion for making superb pork and poultry dishes. It features recipes that are easy to produce, and demonstrates the essentials of what goes into making them.

In the book we'll introduce you to five food heroes who define the food Cranswick is famous for. Martin Heap will share the secrets of his sausages from the original shops around London in the early 1990s, and give you a collection of sausage recipes from around the world using authentic fresh ingredients. Chris Battle, our master curer, will tell his story and explain how we make great traditional dry-cured bacon. Colin Woodall of Cumbria will talk of the long heritage of UK charcuterie and how we have framed this in a modern context. Gill Ridgard tells how to make French all-butter puff pastry. Each of them will then share some of their favourite recipes for their key ingredients and finally Josh Ebsworth, our latest addition to our family, will take us through his smoking techniques and the ultimate barbecue.

Simon Woods, Cranswick's executive development chef, provides a guide to which cuts of pork and chicken to buy and why, and includes some of his favourite recipes from around the world. He lists the traditional butchery techniques for the cuts of meat in the recipes, as well as what to look out for when selecting meat for other recipes.

For the recipes, you'll find a sausage roll next to jerk chicken legs. You'll find KFC (that's Korean Fried Chicken not the other one), next to a classic roast pork with crackling. And you'll find Heap's ultimate sausage and mash next to pork buns and chicken piri piri. There are new cooking methods that will enable you to achieve chef-like results, and new marinades and spices, as well as techniques such as sous vide which enable you to cook pork in a water bath at precise temperatures that give you a consistent result.

In short, you are going to become an expert in pork and chicken so that when you feel like it you can pull out all the stops for your family, your friends and even for the barbecue – there's so much more to discover beyond sausages over hot coals.

Happy reading, happy shopping and above all happy cooking.

GOURMET SAUSAGES
— Martin Heap, Heap's Simply Sausages

Visit a supermarket today and you'll find a bewildering array of sausages both traditional and exotic. Go to the majority of restaurants and you'll find a sausage on the menu taking pride of place. Everybody loves a banger.

But it wasn't always this way. There was a time when the British sausage was at the bottom of the pile. Then Martin Heap, an ex-chef with a vision, decided to open a sausage shop in London's Smithfield Market with a new breed of sausage. From that moment on the landscape shifted and the sausage started its slow rise to stardom.

"It was no eureka moment, I can tell you," Martin explains. "It was in the recession of the early 1990s. Supermarkets were taking over butcher's shops. Dewhurst closed 850 shops almost overnight.

"I had had a restaurant in Greenwich but was looking for a new challenge. So, I took on a butcher's shop in Smithfield and started making sausages in front of my customers. I don't know why. It just seemed right. I had trained as a classical chef with a lot of experience in larder work, which is where all the terrines and pies were made.

"The sausage was not trendy at all but I knew just how to make a classic sausage in the European style using modern ingredients.

"I took an old product and bought good cuts of meat like shoulder and belly from the market that I was a part of and used fresh herbs, fresh vegetables and booze to create a line that people just identified with.

"It was funny but all the old traders came to look at what I was doing. The shop had classic tiled walls and was open so you could see everything. Before long I moved to Berwick Street Market in Soho and then on to other markets.

"The sausage I inherited might have been flavoured with dried sage and onion. I replaced that with fresh sage and caramelised onions. It was a simple idea. I couldn't believe it when I started to supply chefs. I even sold sausages to Albert Roux at Le Gavroche, one of the pinnacles of fine gastronomy, which showed how much food was changing and how the British were proud of their food heritage and wanted a piece of it.

"One day I was approached by Cranswick to start a joint venture. They had the pork, I had the nous, and together we developed what became known as the Sausages of Distinction. We developed the process called mince and mix – you can see the herbs and fresh ingredients in the skin before you start cooking."

TODAY THE SAUSAGE HAS BECOME A MEAL IN A SKIN. IT'S ONE OF THOSE PRODUCTS THAT EVERYBODY LOVES. WHAT I LOVE ABOUT CRANSWICK IS HOW THEY CONSISTENTLY SPOT SMALL BUSINESSES WITH GOOD PRODUCTS AND HELP THEM TO REACH A WIDER AUDIENCE.

BUYING GUIDE

22 — 37

In this book you'll find a number of nutritionally balanced recipes to help you include pork and chicken in your diet. Before you go shopping though, it's worth spending some time considering why these two meats are such valuable components of a healthy and varied diet – not only are they both easy to cook, but they also contain vital nutrients needed to maintain a healthy body and provide a balanced diet.

THE HEALTH BENEFITS
OF WHITE MEAT

White meat generally has a much lower fat content, and is a leaner source of protein with fewer calories, than dark meat. The fat content of pork with its external fat removed, for example, has been reduced considerably over the last 30 years, with modern genetics reducing fat content in lean pork to less than 3%.

The essential vitamins, minerals and protein contained in both meats can all help with controlling your weight, cholesterol and blood pressure.

— Vitamins

Eating a balanced diet that contains pork and chicken will contribute to your recommended daily vitamin intake.

Pork contains:

Vitamin B2 Riboflavin, which helps with energy production in your body and helps your body use other B vitamins,

Vitamin B3 Niacin, a vitamin that helps your body use sugars and fatty acids more efficiently, it produces energy in all body cells, and aids functions in the body such as growth and metabolism, and is a part of the normal functioning of your body's enzymes,

Vitamin B6 Pyridoxine, which helps your body create the amino acids used to make body cells, and contributes to producing vital chemicals including antibodies, haemoglobin and insulin,

Vitamin B12 Cyanocobalamin, which aids blood formation and brain function,

Vitamin D, which increases the amount of calcium and phosphorus your body absorbs from foods.

Chicken contains:

Vitamin A, which helps your body's immune system work properly against illness and infection, helps your vision, and keeps your skin healthy,

Vitamin B1 Thiamine, which has an essential role in body functions and keeps the nervous system healthy,

Vitamin B9 Folic Acid, which helps the body form healthy red blood cells,

Vitamin C, which helps to protect cells and keeps them healthy, maintaining healthy skin, blood vessels, bones and cartilage, and promotes wound healing,

Vitamin D, which helps regulate the amount of calcium and phosphate in the body, needed to keep bones, teeth and muscles healthy,

Vitamin E, which helps maintain healthy skin and eyes, and strengthen the body's immune system against illness and infection,

Vitamin K, which is needed to help wounds heal properly,

and *Vitamins B2, B3, B6 and B12.*

— Minerals

Minerals are the chemical elements found in food that support various functions in your body. Both pork and chicken are naturally low in salt and a good source of other minerals, including:

Iron, which prevents anaemia, fights fatigue, helps metabolise protein and plays a role in the production of haemoglobin and red blood cells. It also builds up the immune system and aids concentration, reduces insomnia and regulates body temperature,

Potassium, which is crucial for general health, helps the kidneys, heart and other organs to function normally, and protects blood vessels,

Phosphorous, which helps body growth and maintenance,

Selenium, which is an essential mineral which prevents common forms of cancer, and defends against heart, autoimmune and thyroid diseases,

Zinc, which is essential for a healthy brain and immune system.

— Protein

White meat is a particularly good source of protein, which is essential for muscle building and the growth, development, structure and function of cells, tissues and organs. If you're looking for meat with low proportions of fat then the leaner cuts of pork will suit your diet. Chicken is a particularly good quality complete protein, containing high levels of amino acids, which are the building blocks for your muscles.

BUYING PORK

When you're buying pork you simply buy the best. Provenance and breeding play an important role in texture and flavour so it's worth hunting down the best you can. Our own pigs are speciality breeds, *Hampshire Cross* or *Breckland White*, reared on our farms. These pigs are all outdoor-bred and live in large, deep, straw-bedded barns that are RSPCA-approved to ensure the highest welfare standards.

The Hampshire Cross is American in origin and chosen for its softer texture and higher levels of intramuscular fat. The Breckland White is a white Duroc breed, a hardy animal that is perfect for rearing outdoors and also carries more fat. Much modern pork has become too lean; these traditional breeds offer superb succulence and flavour.

— Cuts of pork

1 Head
2 Shoulder
3 Belly
4 Loin
5 Leg

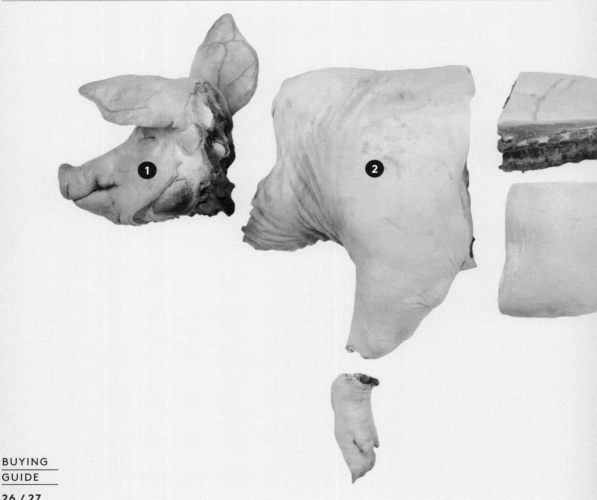

The key to buying pork is to remember this simple rule of thumb: if you want a dish that is light and quick to prepare, then look for a cut that is lean with little fat. A stir-fry, for instance, needs a cut like the tenderloin. This will cook quickly and can be cut into smaller pieces.

However, fat is essential to certain cooking methods. If you're going for roast pork with perfect crackling then you need a crackling boneless loin joint, which has extra fat to deliver the 'crackle' and protect the meat during the longer cooking time. Pork belly also needs to be cooked slowly, and its fat content keeps it moist and succulent. Ultimately the choice is yours but each cut has its place.

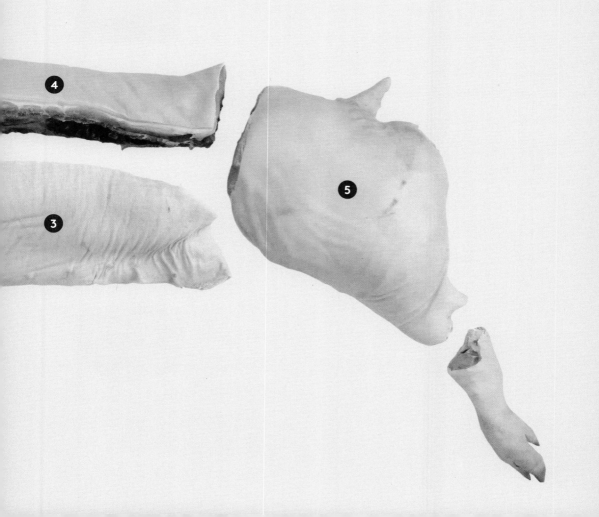

---

❶ Head:

Cheeks — *ideal for slow cooking | sous vide*

This is a fantastic cut of meat from the jowl. Pigs' cheeks have marbled fat running through them and when they're slow cooked they're really tasty and succulent. Because of their size, cheeks are perfect for small plates or starters. The recipe on page 82 cooks them sous vide, they're served with a red wine jus and ultimate mashed potato loaded with clotted cream.

❷ Shoulder:

Neck fillet — *ideal for roasting | slow cooking | smoking | sous vide*

Great for pulled pork because of the marbled fat running through it. The chine side is the prime shoulder cut for roasting, and is also good strung and tied as a joint. The rind can be left on the neck fillet for excellent crackling. The recipe on page 72 is a hog roast joint from the diamond-scored rind-on neck fillet. The joint is stuffed with lemon and sage and then tied back together. When cooked you get a perfect hog roast joint without having to roast a whole pig. Always use outdoor-bred pork for this joint to ensure you get a good depth of fat on the rind to create the perfect crackling.

Chine side of the shoulder, the prime side roasting joint is ideal for slow roasting. Long slow cooking lets the fat render down and the meat tenderise, resulting in a lovely juicy piece of pork that is full of flavour.

Hand side of the shoulder, this is really tasty as a joint, but we tend to use it as the meat for gourmet sausages as well as for pork mince. It's a lean cut with plenty of flavour that works well in the Asian-inspired dishes on pages 138 and 142. Martin Heap created a recipe for the most colourful bangers and mash you'll ever see on page 70, the ultimate sausages, using a mixture of ground pork shoulder and pork belly for succulence. There is only one cooking method for this because they have to be properly cooked – pan-fried on a medium heat. In order to break down the natural casing of the sausage, the sausage needs frying in a little oil until the skins are perfectly brown on all sides. Doing this on a medium heat ensures the sausage is fully cooked through and the outside is perfectly browned.

Boston butt — *ideal for slow cooking | smoking*

This cut originated in America. It's from the upper shoulder with the shoulder blade running through it. When slow cooked the bone conducts heat evenly through the joint and breaks down the collagen to create a great tasting, succulent piece of pork. The recipe on page 126 fuses classic Mexican carnitas with American smoky pulled pork.

❸ Belly:

Square cut belly — *ideal for grilling / roasting / slow cooking / sous vide*

This is a key cut of pork for many modern gastropub dishes, and is used widely throughout Asia. It's best cooked low and slow to allow the meat to become tender and the fat to render down. Ask your butcher to remove the ribs and sternum and cut it square for perfect joints or slices. Pork belly is also a key ingredient for gourmet sausages and dry-cured air-dried bacon. The recipe for toffee apple pork belly on page 52 is cooked sous vide, but with a finishing sauce to allow all the flavours you would normally lose to be captured.

St Louis (King) ribs — *ideal for barbecuing / slow cooking / smoking*

These ribs have the most meat on the bone and are the ultimate barbecue ribs. Go for ribs that have at least 3cm of meat over the bones, and cook them for longer. Our St Louis ribs on page 130 are marinated with ground coffee beans, mustard, allspice and garlic to achieve an authentic American rib. When cooking St Louis ribs in the smoker there are two distinct phases – first the smoking/colouring, then the low and slow cooking. Once you have achieved some good colour by smoking for 2-3 hours, wrap the ribs in foil, reduce the temperature slightly and cook for another 2 hours until tender. By cooking this way you achieve a great colour on the outside and a pink smoke ring on the inside while the meat stays succulent and white.

Individual belly ribs, the rib cage from the belly – gives a bigger piece than the baby back ribs, more suitable for individually cut ribs, but can also be squared off the produce a St Louis rib.

❹ Loin:

Chops — *ideal for barbecuing / pan frying*

Cut between the ribs and with the chine bone removed. A pork chop is traditionally cut between the ribs for a super thick and succulent chop. We've taken this one step further and left the rib bone in, and then French-trimmed the bone to create a pork tomahawk chop. This can be cooked in lots of ways but suits a griddle pan or barbecue best. On page 140 there's a recipe where the chop is cooked in a griddle pan with garlic, thyme and rosemary.

④ Loin:

Rib roast — *ideal for roasting*

The king of pork joints! We take the front end of the loin where the ribs are and remove the chine bone so that you can slice between the ribs individually. This cut carries a little fat at the shoulder end, which helps keep it succulent and tender. It's served either rind-on or rindless. Leave it rind-on for perfect crackling, and diamond-score it for a stunning roast. The important thing to remember is to be really careful not to overcook it – use a meat thermometer and you can't go wrong! On page 68 there's a rib of pork recipe for perfect crackling. You need to deeply score the rind through the fat, but not into the meat, and pour freshly boiled water over the top to open up the scoring. Dry the pork, and then rub it with olive oil and sprinkle with lots of salt. Roast it in the oven for 45 minutes at 230°C – this allows the crackling to pop and achieve a golden bubbly crust. Then turn the oven down low until the temperature reaches 70°C. Finally rest the meat for 15 minutes to allow it to relax before slicing and serving.

Crackling boneless loin joint — *ideal for roasting*

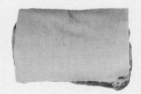

Crackling is one of the most loved parts of pork, yet people tell me they can't get the rind to crackle. You simply need to start with the right meat – you need at least 14mm of fat cover, deeply scored. Take a whole boneless pork joint and carefully score it in rows ½cm apart, to enable easy slicing and portioning once cooked, being careful to cut all the way through the rind but not into the fat. It's then cooked in the same way as the rib roast above. There's a recipe for a rosemary-roasted loin joint on page 80 where you slice open the joint and sprinkle in a seasoned rosemary mix to enhance the flavour, before tying it back up and roasting it in the oven.

Baby back (loin) ribs — *ideal for barbecuing | slow cooking | smoking*

These are the prime ribs favoured by the American market for their consistency and succulent tender meat. The secret to perfecting these is to peel off the membrane from the back of the ribs to allow your marinade to penetrate the meat from both sides. On page 128 there's a recipe where the ribs are cooked on a smoker on a low heat before being basted in char siu sauce for perfect dark and sticky glazed ribs.

Rib eye — *ideal for barbecuing | pan frying*

Pork rib eye has similar characteristics to beef rib eye. It delivers great flavour and succulence because of the fat content. I love to cook rib eye steaks simply with butter and sage sous vide to 56°C, then finish them by pan frying with a generous sprinkling of sea salt and cracked black pepper.

Tenderloin (fillet) — *ideal for pan frying / sous vide*

An underrated cut of meat in the UK, it's super-lean and is perfect for quick and easy healthy dishes. There are two great recipes using tenderloin in the book, in the first on page 44 there's a lovely pork and black pudding Wellington, and in the second on page 98 it's wrapped in Woodall's Black Combe ham and served with Calvados jus.

Fillet noisette — *ideal for pan frying*

A superb cut of meat to make delicate healthy dishes. Simply slice the whole tenderloin into 2cm slices and pan-fry in a little oil over a high heat. The recipe for Indonesian pork fillet satay on page 146 is very quick to make and super healthy.

Leg:

Leg joint — *ideal for curing /roasting*

The traditional Sunday roast joint, with a good amount of fat it will crackle beautifully. It must be deeply scored through the rind and into the fat, but not the meat. The leg is also cured to make gammon. For the East meets West recipe on page 66 you marinate a gammon joint in soy, ginger, chilli, garlic and maple syrup, and serve it with a classic English parsley sauce.

Topside — *ideal for pan frying*

A very lean piece of meat that should be sliced thinly and cooked quickly. It's ideal for stir-fries or quick-cook sizzle steaks, cooked for just a minute either side. On page 166 there's a quick and easy recipe for Thai red curry using thinly-cut topside strips. The pork gives great flavour and texture as well as being super-quick to cook.

Shank — *ideal for curing / slow cooking / sous vide*

A rindless 'spoon bone' cut is a great way to serve shanks. For the recipe by Colin Woodall on page 76 you dry cure the meat for 4 days before marinating it in honey and spices. The 'spoon bone' cut is pork's equivalent to lamb shanks and is the perfect size for one person. When slow cooked the bone twists straight out and leaves 100% gammon.

Hock — *ideal for curing / slow cooking*

The hock has been used for curing and slow cooking for decades. It's not as appealing as the shank for presentation, so it's normally pulled off the bone once cooked and used for making terrines. There's a fantastic recipe on page 108 for a ham hock and caper terrine.

BUYING CHICKEN

We all remember chicken that really tasted of chicken. We recreate this flavour with slower-grown breeds of free-range corn-fed birds. Our chickens are reared on our own farms in and around Norfolk which contributes significantly to the meat quality. Food miles are key to preserving sustainable food production and the environment.

There are two main types of chicken. The first is free range, these slower-growing birds from specific breeds are reared outdoors during the day and protected indoors at night. The longer the chicken develops, the more the flavour intensifies. However, it also means that muscle fibres are more developed which gives the meat a firmer texture. This is an important consideration when it comes to cooking.

The second type of bird is a high-welfare Red Tractor breed, which is raised indoors and achieves a desired weight faster. This process produces birds that are more delicate and tender, which many consumers prefer. This type of chicken is also much cheaper – sometimes as much as half the price of a free-range bird.

With pork, the secret lies in the amount of fat in each cut, but chicken is naturally not as fatty. Remove the skin and the meat is almost uniformly lean. Like pork this can be an advantage in quick cooking. However, for slow cooking, such as a roast, the fat plays an important part. What you really need to take care with is the moisture content. Keeping the skin on to protect the chicken whilst cooking helps to keep the moisture in and produces succulent meat.

French housewives have an expression that goes 'always choose a mad chicken'. What they mean is that the best-flavoured meat comes from a bird that has worked its legs by running around a lot. The most flavoursome part of a chicken is the legs, so thighs and drumsticks are the best cuts for flavour. The breast is more tender and lean and needs more attention when cooking. There are recipes in the book that take advantage of each cut's properties and celebrate their different flavours.

Whole chicken — *ideal for barbecuing / roasting*

As with all meat, you need to buy the best you can: look out for free-range or British Red Tractor chicken. The recipe on page 64 uses a free-range corn-fed chicken stuffed with lemon and sage, with garlic and herb butter massaged under the skin to create a mouthwatering bird that is juicy and succulent when carved. Don't be scared to have a go at butchering your own chicken, it's easy and takes no time at all. It can be quickly cut into breasts, thighs, drumsticks and wings as in the recipes for coq au vin on page 62, and piri piri chicken on page 156.

Breast — *ideal for barbecuing | pan frying | roasting | sous vide*

The most widely used cut of chicken, but unfortunately sometimes the only cut people eat because of its lean white meat and ease of cooking. A supreme is a breast with the skin is left on, which adds flavour, especially if you are cooking with a corn-fed bird. There are lots of recipes using chicken breast in the book, including a recipe for chicken burritos with lime rice on page 134, where the chicken is slow cooked, a technique perfect for achieving flavoursome hot pulled chicken. There's also a fantastic wrapped chicken breast dish using 'nduja and Woodall's pancetta on page 78. If spicy food isn't your thing try the classic chicken Kiev coated in crisp panko breadcrumbs on page 86.

Inner fillet — *ideal for pan frying*

The tenderest cut, taken from the bottom of the breast. As with pork fillet, the chicken inner fillet is best cooked on a high temperature for a short amount of time. The recipe on page 100 pairs fillets with spicy Cumberland salami crisps and pea and mint purée – a great small plate or starter which is quick and easy to prepare.

Thigh fillet — *ideal for barbecuing | deep frying | pan frying | roasting*

A superbly flavoursome piece of meat which works well for many recipes in this book. Thighs are very popular in Asian cooking – and taste like proper chicken! Leg meat on chicken is now almost as white as the breast, but it still delivers much more flavour. Thigh meat would be my cut of choice because like breast it can be cooked in every possible way achieving different flavours and textures, but it delivers extra flavour. One of my favourite recipes in the book is KFC on page 150 – 'K' being Korean! The thighs are marinated in Korean spices and buttermilk, which tenderises the meat, and then coated and deep-fried.

Legs & drumsticks — *ideal for barbecuing | roasting*

Wonderfully tasty pieces of meat. Whole legs are ideal for jerk chicken, and cooking on the bone develops the flavour and tenderness of the meat. There's a great jerk chicken recipe on page 148 using the legs, the key to which is scoring the skin and meat with a knife before marinating.

Wings — *ideal for deep frying | roasting*

A classic of American cuisine: 1.3 billion wings are consumed on Super Bowl weekend alone! There are two key cuts, the mids and primes. There's a great chicken lollipop recipe that uses both cuts on page 116. We turn the meat inside out on the wing bone to create a mini drumstick, then marinate in soy, honey garlic, ginger, lime and chilli.

GOURMET BACON
— Chris Battle, Jack Scaife

The Brits' love of bacon is part of the national identity. Our mission has always been to get the best into supermarkets across the land, bringing a smile to the nation's face.

When Yorkshire butcher Chris Battle took over Jack Scaife's in Keighley in the 1970s, he recalls "One day an old customer walked into the shop, he said that his bacon was no good and what had happened to the bacon of old?

"I remember that we used to say that it was part of the modern curing process. But that only worked for a while. So, when this old boy said what he did, I knew the time was up and it was time to do something about it.

"The problem was that we were all buying Danish bacon at the time. This was a great product when it first arrived as it had started out as a leaner bacon with less salt. It was popular and consistent, but over time the quality had deteriorated as more and more water was injected into it.

"My dilemma was that I couldn't just go back to the curing recipes I had been taught as an apprentice. The old bacon came from pigs that were now rare or extinct and had been extremely fatty. Yes, the bacon fried differently, but it was full of fat. The modern pigs that had taken their place were now smaller and leaner and would not react to the same cure. Everything had changed.

"The next problem was that the cure recipe contained ingredients that were now illegal! So, I had to come up with a completely new cure and a different ageing process. It was a proper conundrum but I relished the challenge because I wanted to eat that same old bacon again and I didn't want to let my customers down.

"I took sides of bacon and used a salt cure and hung them up to dry and tested them out on my customers. It took two years of experimentation before the first positive comments started to come back. Before long, by listening to what my customers wanted, I achieved a crispy bacon that didn't have any of the watery nature of commercial bacon. It could be fried just the way it had once been, but it was leaner and less salty.

"My customers loved it. Almost overnight the business became a bacon shop and we regularly sold out. Not long after that we had some good local press and then I was selling bacon to Fortnum & Mason and the House of Lords. Modern dry-cure bacon had been reinvented.

"We started to do mail order and pretty soon were selling bacon all over the world, particularly to ex-pats who wanted a taste of home. By the 1990s the mail order business had started to go online and my daughter recommended the internet. It was slow at first but it caught on."

TODAY I STILL ENJOY
THE CURING PROCESS.
I'M STILL EXPERIMENTING
WITH DIFFERENT SALTS
AND DIFFERENT CUTS.
IT REALLY IS AMAZING
WHAT HAPPENS WHEN
YOU ACCEPT THAT
THINGS AREN'T WHAT
THEY USED TO BE AND
YOU DECIDE TO DO
SOMETHING ABOUT IT.

MODERN CLASSICS

38 — 89

PERFECT PASTRY

— Gill Ridgard, Yorkshire Baker

A sausage roll consists of two things: sausage meat and puff pastry. So, why are they so difficult to make properly? Gill Ridgard, pioneer and founder of Yorkshire Baker, understands all too well. She's been making them for many years.

"The simple things are the hardest to make," she explains. "The reason is that you can't hide. Every ingredient, every technique and every process must be perfect, otherwise the customer will know the difference and they won't pay the price.

"I grew up as a farmer's daughter and trained as a butcher. I remember vividly the food we used to make at home and it always tasted fantastic. My family had a farm shop and I wanted to have a business that could offer simple foods like sausage rolls that had that distinctive home taste.

"Sausage meat I could do with my eyes closed. As a butcher I knew what cuts of pork worked best and what ratio of fat and meat made the perfect sausage meat. I didn't want any gristle or cheap carcass meat in my sausage rolls. I wanted the best.

"However, I had to learn the pastry side, which I got from some chef friends, and then it was all about finding the right ingredients.

"This is where the good sausage roll and the mediocre separate. The really good ones use the right flour and only butter. I was using a flour from France but was being prohibited by cost until a local grower came to see me saying he was growing the same flour in Yorkshire using the same seed: the soissons. So now all our flour comes from Yorkshire, which I'm really proud of because it adds to our story and makes us more local and regional.

"The only other major ingredients are the all-important butter and water but I soon discovered that there was a fourth, secret, ingredient: time. Great puff pastry needs to be rested; it adds that extra something. The natural yeasts develop flavour. Our sausage rolls take two-and-half days to make which adds additional costs to the process. This is what makes our products different and better.

"What I love is the fact that through my partnership with Cranswick I have taken a simple idea that drew on my roots as a farmer's daughter and included my butchery training."

THE RESULT, BY STICKING
TO MY PRINCIPLES OF
'HOMEMADE TASTES
BEST', IS A BUSINESS THAT
CREATES OUTSTANDING
PRODUCTS THAT ARE
AVAILABLE TO A VERY
WIDE RANGE OF PEOPLE.

BRECKLAND WHITE PORK FILLET AND BLACK PUDDING WELLINGTON

Serves 4: prep: 2 hours *(plus resting)*/cook: *45-50 minutes*

To make the pastry, sift 500g of flour, then rub into it 100g of butter until there are no more lumps. Mix the salt, vinegar and 450ml of cold water, then add to the flour mix and knead for about 3 minutes to form a slack dough. Place it in a bowl, cover with cling film and rest for 1 hour in the fridge. Roll out the rest of the butter between two sheets of silicone paper into a square about ¾cm thick. Rest at room temperature.

Roll out the rested dough, using plenty of flour on the workbench, to just over double the size of the butter. Peel away a piece of silicone from the butter and place it, butter side down, to one side of the dough. Peel the second piece of silicone away, and fold over the dough to envelop the butter. Push down firmly on the edges of the dough to stop the butter escaping whilst rolling. Using more flour dusted on both the bench and the pastry, roll out the pastry to three times its current length. Fold one third over, followed by the other third on top of the first two folds. Place on a tray, cover with cling film and rest in the fridge for at least 1 hour. Turn the pastry 90 degrees and roll out again to three times its length. Repeat the folding process. Rest again for at least 1 hour. Repeat the process another 4 times (a total of 6 times). Return to the fridge, covered in cling film, until needed.

To make the pancakes, crack the eggs into a mixing bowl with the oil and half the milk and lightly whisk, then add the flour and mix until lump-free. Now add the rest of the flour and the salt. Sieve the batter then add the sage to the mix. Heat a large non-stick frying pan on a high heat. Add the butter and allow to colour before adding some of the batter (stir the batter before adding to the pan). Make sure the batter covers the base of the pan evenly and turn to a medium heat. Once it starts to colour around the edges try and free the edges using a spatula and gently flip onto the other side for a final minute before transferring to greaseproof paper for later. Prepare 2 pancakes.

To make the farce, heat the butter in a pan then add the onion and fry on a medium heat for 3-4 minutes. Add the red wine and garlic and continue cooking for a further 4-5 minutes. Add the mushrooms and cover with a lid, allow to slowly cook for a further 5 minutes on a low heat. Remove the lid and allow any excess moisture to cook out before crumbling in the black pudding in. Stir in and remove from the heat; season with salt and freshly cracked black pepper. Allow to cool, then place in the fridge.

for the pastry
600g strong flour
500g unsalted butter
1 tbsp salt
2 tsps malt vinegar

for the pancakes
1 egg and 1 yolk
1 tbsp oil
150ml milk
50g plain flour
¼ tsp salt
1 tbsp fresh sage, finely chopped
20g butter

for the farce
20g butter
100g onion, diced
2 tbsps red wine
3 cloves garlic, peeled and finely diced
100g mushrooms, finely diced
200g black pudding
sea salt & black pepper

for the red wine jus
250g shallots, peeled and finely diced
4 tbsps olive oil
1 garlic clove, peeled and finely diced
1 sprig thyme, leaves only
5 tbsps balsamic vinegar
250ml red wine
400ml chicken stock
50g butter
sea salt & black pepper

for the Wellington
450g Breckland white pork fillet
2 tbsps vegetable oil
sea salt & black pepper
flour, for dusting
1 egg, beaten

To make the red wine jus, heat a saucepan on a medium heat and gently fry the onions in the olive oil until lightly caramelised, then stir in the garlic and thyme. Pour in the vinegar and reduce, then add the red wine and reduce again. Add the chicken stock and reduce by two-thirds, remove from the heat and sieve into a clean pan. Just before serving, bring the sauce to the boil and add the butter, stirring all the time until incorporated, and season with salt and freshly cracked black pepper.

To make the Wellington, once you've made all the components, heat a little vegetable oil in a frying pan over a high heat. Season the pork with salt and freshly cracked black pepper and quick fry until golden in colour, and allow to cool. When cool, lay the pancake on a workbench and cover generously and evenly with the black pudding farce. Place the pork on top of the farce in the middle of the pancake. Gently fold the pancake over the pork and roll the pancake away from you keeping a firm grip and folding the sides of the pancake over the ends of the pork until you form a parcel (this will help hold in the moisture and prevent the pastry going soggy).

Lightly dust the work surface and roll out the pastry into a large rectangle about 5mm thick. Brush the edges of the pastry with beaten egg and lightly in the centre to help it bind to the parcel and keep the moisture in. Place the parcel on the edge of the pastry and roll away from you, make sure you crimp all the edges and place the seam at the bottom trimming any excess pastry. Transfer to a tray lined with greaseproof paper and refrigerate (this stage can be done in advance and refrigerated, but allow 2 hours back at room temperature before cooking).

Pre-heat the oven to 200°C/400°F/gas mark 6. Brush the parcel with beaten egg. Place the tray with the Wellington on it on top of the hob and cook on a high heat for 3-4 minutes to help avoid a soggy base (be careful not to burn it). Bake in the oven for 35-45 minutes. Check the temperature using a meat thermometer – to avoid overcooking you want the centre of the pork to reach 68°C. Remove from the oven, transfer to a wire rack and rest for 5 minutes.

To serve, place the Wellington on a chopping board and using a sharp serrated knife cut the Wellington into 2cm thick slices.

PORK, APPLE AND BLACK PUDDING SAUSAGE ROLL

for the pastry
600g strong flour
500g unsalted butter
1 tbsp salt
2 tsps malt vinegar

for the filling
35g butter
2 medium onions, finely diced
500g pork mince (10% fat)
250g smoked back bacon,
     finely chopped
150g fresh breadcrumbs
100g Bramley apple, peeled and diced
125g black pudding, diced
½ tsp cracked black pepper
1 tsp salt
1 tsp nutmeg
1 tbsp fresh thyme, finely chopped
1 tbsp flat leaf parsley, finely chopped
1 tbsp fresh sage, finely chopped
1 tbsp clear honey
1 tsp Marmite

for the topping
2 medium eggs, whisked together
2 tbsps oats
1 tbsp black onion seeds

for the hog beans
1 tbsp vegetable oil
1 small red onion, finely chopped
80g smoked bacon lardons
40g soft dark brown sugar
30ml red wine vinegar
400g Heinz baked beans
15g butter
sea salt & black pepper

to serve
1 small bottle HP sauce

Makes 12: prep: 1 hour 30 minutes *(plus resting)*/cook: 30-40 minutes

To make the pastry, sift 500g of flour, then rub into it 100g of butter until there are no more lumps. Mix the salt, vinegar and 450ml of cold water, then add to the flour mix and knead for about 3 minutes to form a slack dough. Place it in a bowl, cover with cling film and rest for 1 hour in the fridge. Roll out the rest of the butter between two sheets of silicone paper into a square about ¾cm thick. Rest at room temperature.

Roll out the rested dough, using plenty of flour on the workbench, to just over double the size of the butter. Peel away a piece of silicone from the butter and place it, butter side down, to one side of the dough. Peel the second piece of silicone away, and fold over the dough to envelop the butter. Push down firmly on the edges of the dough to stop the butter escaping whilst rolling. Using more flour dusted on both the bench and the pastry, roll out the pastry to three times its length. Fold one third over, followed by the other third on top of the first two folds. Place on a tray, cover with cling film and rest in the fridge for at least 1 hour. Turn the pastry 90 degrees and roll out again to three times its length. Repeat the folding process. Rest again for at least 1 hour. Repeat the process another 4 times (a total of 6 times). Return to the fridge, covered in cling film, until needed.

To make the sausage roll filling, on a medium heat warm a frying pan until hot, add the butter and onions and gently cook until golden brown. When cooked remove from the heat and allow to cool. When the onions are cool, thoroughly mix all the filling ingredients together in a bowl and cover with cling film. Let the filling stand for 1 hour at room temperature. Put the filling into a disposable piping bag.

To make the sausage rolls, roll the pastry into a rectangle about 2.5mm thick: use plenty of flour so the pastry does not stick. Using a sharp knife cut the pastry into 3 strips around 300mm by 100mm. Cut a hole in the end of the piping bag a little larger than a 50p coin. Pipe the mix into the middle of the strips of pastry. Using a pastry brush and the two whisked eggs, egg wash the edges and fold over the pastry to create the sausage roll. Using a fork push lightly down on the edges to seal. Cut the sausage roll into 100mm lengths and score the top of each 3 times to reveal the filling. Place on a baking tray, egg wash the sausage rolls and sprinkle with the oats and onion seeds. Pre-heat the oven to 180°C/350°F/gas mark 4. Place the tray in the oven and bake for 25-30 minutes until they are a deep golden brown colour. Allow them to rest for 10 minutes before serving.

For the hog beans, heat the vegetable oil in a saucepan and fry off the red onion and lardons until softened and starting to turn brown. Add the sugar, vinegar and beans and bring to a simmer. Before serving add the butter, season with salt and freshly cracked black pepper and mix to create a creamy smooth sauce.

To serve, place the sausage rolls on a plate with a bowl of hog beans, and serve with a good helping of HP Sauce.

QUICHE LORRAINE WITH DRY-CURED STREAKY BACON

Serves 4: prep: 20 minutes/marinate: 3 hours/cook: 1 hour 10 minutes

To make the pastry, put the flour and butter into a bowl and with your fingertips rub together until it begins to look like breadcrumbs. Add the thyme, salt and onions and work for another minute. Add the water and bring together to form a ball. Wrap the pastry in cling film and refrigerate for 2 hours. Remove the pastry from the cling film and on a floured surface roll out to a 2mm thick circle, big enough to cover a 20cm x 5cm tart ring. Line a flat baking tray with greaseproof paper and place the 20cm ring on top. Roll the pastry around your rolling pin, then gently lay it on top of the ring. Work the pastry into the base of the ring before trimming off any excess. Refrigerate for another hour.

Pre-heat the oven to 180°C/350°F/gas mark 4. Remove the lined ring from the fridge and cover with greaseproof paper. Place a layer of baking beans on top of the greaseproof paper, place in the oven and blind bake for 20-25 minutes. Remove from the oven and carefully remove the baking beans and greaseproof paper; leave to cool.

To make the cheese filling, mix all the cheeses, bacon and seasoning together in a bowl. Place the cheese mix into the cooked pastry case.

To make the custard, crack the eggs into a mixing bowl and pour in the milk and cream then whisk together. Pour the custard over the cheese mix in the pastry case until it's 1cm from the top of the pastry.

To make the bacon topping, cut a circle of greaseproof paper the same size as your tart tin. Lay out 4 slices of bacon on greaseproof paper and weave another 4 slices through them to create a lattice. Gently turn over the greaseproof paper and place it on top of the custard in the tart tin. Peel the paper off leaving the bacon lattice on top of the quiche.

To cook the quiche, pre-heat the oven to 150°C/300°F/gas mark 3. Place the quiche in the oven and bake for 25-30 minutes until the custard has set and the streaky bacon is golden brown. Stand for 20 minutes at room temperature, then slice and serve.

for the pastry
500g plain flour
250g unsalted butter, diced
1 tbsp fresh thyme, roughly chopped
1 heaped tsp salt
100g dried kibbled onions
125ml water

for the filling
100g Comté cheese, grated
100g Gruyère cheese, grated
50g Parmesan cheese, grated
150g smoked streaky bacon, chopped, cooked
1 pinch of whole nutmeg, grated
1 pinch of cracked black pepper

for the custard
6 free range eggs
250ml double cream
250ml whole milk

for the bacon topping
120g dry-cured smoked streaky bacon

BLACKSTICKS BLUE CHICKEN CORDON BLEU WITH FENNEL-ROASTED POTATOES

for the chicken

4 x 150g boneless skinless
chicken breasts
80g wholegrain mustard
4 slices of smoked dry-cured ham
320g Blacksticks Blue cheese
100g plain flour, seasoned with salt
and cracked black pepper
2 eggs
200g panko breadcrumbs

for the fennel-roasted potatoes

600g Charlotte potatoes
1 bulb of fennel, thick sliced
6 cloves garlic, skin on
8 sprigs of fresh thyme
5 sprigs of fresh rosemary
80ml extra virgin olive oil
sea salt & black pepper

Serves 4: prep: 30 minutes/cook: 45 minutes

To cook the chicken, in between two sheets of cling film flatten out the breasts to approximately 7mm thick: try to keep as much of a round shape as possible to make the final dish more presentable. Lay the breasts out and spread 20g of wholegrain mustard evenly on top of each one, followed by a slice of ham. Thinly slice the Blacksticks Blue (tip: use a cheese wire if you have one, or a knife that has been dipped in hot water and then dried in between each slice). Divide the cheese evenly and lay on top of the ham. Roll up the chicken, tucking in the ends to give a thick even piece.

Wrap the rolls in cling film and refrigerate for at least 1 hour. Put the seasoned flour, egg and panko breadcrumbs into three dishes. Roll the chicken in the seasoned flour ensuring it is totally coated. Do the same with the egg and finish in the breadcrumbs, making sure each breast is coated evenly.

Pre-heat the oven to 180°C/350°F/gas mark 4. Heat a generous amount of sunflower oil in a non-stick frying pan over a medium heat; when very hot cook the chicken for 1½ minutes on each side, turning when golden brown to fully cook the outside coating. Place on a baking tray and bake in the oven for 20 minutes until cooked through.

To cook the fennel-roasted potatoes, pre-heat the oven to 200°C/400°F/gas mark 6. Slice the Charlotte potatoes in half (try and get them roughly the same size so they cook evenly) and place in a baking tray. Add the sliced fennel and mix with the potatoes. Mix in the skin-on garlic cloves, thyme and rosemary sprigs, olive oil and season with a large pinch of salt and freshly cracked black pepper, place in the pre-heated oven for 45 minutes, turning occasionally.

To serve, slice the chicken evenly into 5-6 slices and serve with the fennel-roasted potatoes.

BRECKLAND WHITE PORK BELLY WITH TOFFEE APPLE SAUCE

Serves 4: prep: 20 minutes/sous vide: 14 hours/cook: 30-40 minutes

To make the stock, heat a pan on a medium heat with a little oil and lightly fry the ginger and chilli. Add the crumbled pork stock cube, water, soy sauce and cinnamon and bring to the boil.

To make the toffee apple sauce, once the stock has boiled turn down the heat to medium. Add the spices, apple sauce, grated apple, soy sauce and sugars and dissolve the sugar gently by stirring over a low heat. When dissolved bring to the boil and thicken with the cornflour mixed in the water. Cook out for another 2 minutes, and chill down the sauce.

To cook the pork belly, preset your sous vide machine to 85°C. Place the pork belly and sauce in a vacuum bag and seal. Place the sealed bag into the sous vide machine and set the timer for 14 hours. When cooked the pork can be rapid-chilled (submerge the bag in icy water to reduce the temperature quickly) or, if using straight away, pre-heat the oven to 200°C/400°F/gas mark 6. Remove the belly from the bag, place on a baking tray and roast for 25-30 minutes until caramelised and golden brown. Pour the sauce from the bag into a saucepan and reduce to a thick, double-cream-like consistency.

To cook the pork belly (without a sous vide machine), pre-heat the oven to 140°C/275°F/gas mark 1. Place the pork belly and toffee apple sauce into a deep casserole dish. Cover with tin foil and cook in the oven for 3 hours. Remove from the oven, discard the foil and carefully pour off the juices into a pan. Turn the oven up to 180°c/350°F/gas mark 4 and cook for 30-35 minutes until the belly is golden brown. Reduce the sauce by half on a medium heat to a thick sauce the consistency of double cream.

To make ultimate mash, place the potatoes in a pan of cold water with a pinch of salt. Bring to the boil and simmer for 15-20 minutes until very tender. Whilst the potatoes are cooking heat up the cream and butter with a pinch of salt and pepper; when the butter has melted, stir in and remove from the heat. When the potato is cooked pass through a ricer into a bowl. Mix the butter and cream mixture through, season with salt and pepper.

To caramelise the apple, melt the butter in a frying pan. Add the sugar and cinnamon and mix together on a medium heat. Add the apples and fry until the sugar caramelises and looks golden brown. Turn the apples, and cook for another minute, then remove from the caramel and set aside.

To char the broccoli, place the broccoli in a bowl, drizzle with the olive oil and sprinkle with a large pinch of salt and freshly cracked black pepper. Ensure it has been fully coated in the olive oil. Heat a griddle pan over a high heat and bring to smoking point. Add the broccoli and cook for 90 seconds on each side until it is crunchy with charred edges.

To serve, spoon the mash onto a large dish and top with the broccoli. Slice the pork belly into 1cm thick slices and lay on top. Finish with the caramelised apple and drizzle with the toffee apple sauce.

for the spiced pork stock
1 small lobe of ginger, peeled and grated
½ red chilli, chopped and seeds removed
1 pork stock cube
450ml water
50ml dark soy sauce
1 cinnamon stick

for the toffee apple sauce
500ml spiced pork stock
½ tsp Chinese five-spice
½ tsp mustard seeds
½ tsp fennel seeds
75g Bramley apple sauce
1 Bramley apple, grated
50g molasses sugar
50g light soy sauce
50g light muscavado sugar
50g dark muscavado sugar
20g cornflour
25g cold water

for the pork belly
1kg Breckland rindless pork belly

for ultimate mash
1kg Maris Piper potatoes, peeled and chopped into evenly-sized pieces
90g clotted cream
100g unsalted butter
sea salt & white pepper

for the caramelised apple
60g butter
60g caster sugar
1 pinch of cinnamon
2 Jazz apples, topped and tailed and sliced into 1.5 cm thick slices

for the charred broccoli
250g tenderstem broccoli
2 tbsps olive oil
sea salt & black pepper

CHARGRILLED CHICKEN BREAST AND LITTLE GEM LETTUCE WITH BLACKSTICKS BLUE DRESSING

for the marinade

4 boneless chicken breasts, skinless
250ml buttermilk
1 lime, zest and juice
2 tsps garlic powder
2 tsps smoked paprika
1 tsp ground coriander
1 tsp ground cumin
½ tsp turmeric
2 tsps of hot sauce, tabasco or similar
1 tsp granulated sugar
1 tsp cracked black pepper
1 tbsp fresh coriander,
  roughly chopped
2 tsps salt

for cooking the chicken

2 tbsps vegetable oil
sea salt & black pepper

for the blue cheese dressing

120g Blacksticks Blue
  cheese, crumbled
180ml soured cream
50g mayonnaise
1 tsp English mustard
1 tsp lemon juice
2 tbsps of cider vinegar
1 tsp Worcester sauce
sea salt & black pepper

for the croutons

1 uncut loaf of sourdough bread
  (a day old is best)
2 tbsps of light olive oil
½ tsp cracked black pepper

for the lettuce

4 Little Gem lettuces, cut in half,
  washed and dried
olive oil
1 tbsp chives, finely chopped

Serves 4: prep: 20 minutes/marinate: 4 hours/cook: 20-25 minutes

To make the marinade, in a large bowl whisk together all the ingredients except the chicken. Pour the marinade into a large sealable plastic bag, add the chicken, seal the bag and refrigerate for 4 hours.

To cook the chicken, pre-heat a griddle pan on a medium heat. Remove the chicken from the marinade and pat dry with paper towels. Brush the chicken with oil and season with salt and freshly ground black pepper to taste on both sides. Griddle for 12-15 minutes, turning halfway through, until golden brown and charred on both sides and the chicken has reached 75°C at the thickest point of the breast using your food meat thermometer. Place the chicken on a warm plate to rest for 5 minutes before slicing.

To make the blue cheese dressing, whilst the chicken is resting place all the ingredients in a blender or food processor, reserving 50g of the cheese, and blend for a few seconds. Check the seasoning and adjust to your taste with salt and freshly cracked black pepper. The dressing can be stored in an airtight container in the fridge for up to 1 week.

For the croutons, pre-heat the oven to 190°C/375°F/gas mark 5. Remove the outer crust from the uncut sourdough loaf and pull into pieces (don't worry if the pieces are different sizes, they'll look more natural when plated). Sprinkle with olive oil, season lightly with pepper and bake until golden and crisp (around 10 minutes). These can be made up to a day in advance and kept in an airtight container.

To fry the lettuce, place a griddle pan on a high heat. Brush the cut side of the Little Gem lettuce with olive oil and place, cut side down, on the griddle pan and fry for a few seconds to colour – don't grill for more than 1 minute.

To serve, arrange the sliced chicken over the lettuce, drizzle over some of the blue cheese dressing and sprinkle the remaining cheese and some of the croutons. Finish with the chives and serve immediately.

CHICKEN SAUSAGE
SUPERFOOD SALAD

Serves 4: prep: 20 minutes/cook: 45 minutes

To make the salad, place the quinoa in a sieve and wash thoroughly under cold water. Place in a pan with 400g of cold water, the dried basil and the sundried tomato paste. Mix well to dissolve the tomato paste in the water, season with salt and freshly cracked black pepper, place over a medium heat and bring to the boil. Reduce the heat and simmer for 15-20 minutes, stirring occasionally, until all the liquid has been absorbed into the quinoa. Once cooked fluff up with a fork ready for serving.

Place the giant couscous in another saucepan with 150ml of water, season with salt and cracked black pepper and bring to the boil over a medium heat. Stir, place a lid on the pan and turn off the heat. Leave for 15 minutes for the couscous to absorb all the liquid, then fluff up with a fork. Pre-heat the oven to 180°C/350°F/gas mark 4, place the diced butternut squash on a non-stick tray and drizzle over the olive oil. Season with salt and cracked black pepper and place in the oven for 15 minutes. Remove from the oven, add the broccoli and beetroot to the tray, turn the vegetables over with a fish slice to coat in the oil and return to the oven for another 12 minutes.

For the sausages, place a griddle pan over a medium heat. Place the sausages in a bowl and drizzle with the vegetable oil to fully coat, then place the sausages in the pan and cook, turning every 2 minutes for a total of 12 minutes until they are golden brown and the skins are crisp.

To serve, in a large bowl mix the giant couscous, quinoa and roasted vegetables together gently, add the avocado and basil and gently mix again. Place a large scoop of the salad mixture on a plate, add a tablespoon of pomegranate seeds and the sunflower seeds, sprinkle with chopped parsley and drizzle with the olive oil. Top with two chicken sausages.

for the salad
200g quinoa
1 tsp dried basil
40g sundried tomato paste
sea salt & black pepper
100g giant couscous
*1 butternut squash, peeled,
    seeds removed, diced*
3 tbsps olive oil
180g tenderstem broccoli
*150g beetroot, precooked,
    roughly diced*
*1 avocado, peeled, stone
    removed, diced*
20g fresh basil, roughly chopped

for the sausages
8 chicken sausages
1 tbsp vegetable oil

to serve
1 pomegranate, seeds removed
60g pumpkin seeds, toasted
2 tbsps olive oil
*20g fresh flat leaf parsley,
    roughly chopped*

CIDER-MARINATED PORK LOIN STEAKS WITH CHARRED APPLE AND FENNEL SALAD

for the pork

*4 x 160g Hampshire pork
  loin medallions*
120ml pear cider
2 tbsps vegetable oil

for the salad

*2 Pink Lady apples, cored and cut
  into 8 wedges*
*1 large head fennel, cored and cut
  into large pieces*
4 tbsps olive oil
sea salt & black pepper
*20g fresh flat leaf parsley,
  roughly chopped*

for the blackberry vinaigrette

150g blackberries
30g cider vinegar
20g balsamic vinegar
50g pear cider
20g honey

to serve

1 tbsp olive oil

Serves 4: prep: 20 minutes/marinate: 2-6 hours/cook: 15 minutes

To cook the pork, in a bowl mix the pork loin medallions and pear cider, cover, and refrigerate for 2-6 hours. Heat a griddle pan over a medium heat until smoking hot. Remove the pork from the cider and place on a baking tray. Drizzle the vegetable oil over the medallions ensuring they are evenly covered. Place the medallions in the griddle pan and cook for 2 minutes then turn over. Repeat for 3 more turns, cooking for 8 minutes in total. Transfer the medallions to a warm plate to rest for 4 minutes before serving.

To make the salad, heat a griddle pan on a high heat. Toss the apples and fennel in half of the olive oil and season with a large pinch of salt and freshly cracked black pepper. Add the apples and fennel to the pan and stir every 2 minutes until charred and slightly softened. When cooked add the parsley and remaining half of olive oil.

For the blackberry vinaigrette, add all of the ingredients to a food processor and blend to a smooth sauce.

To serve, place a pile of the apple and fennel salad on a plate, top with a pork steak and drizzle with the olive oil and blackberry vinaigrette.

CITRUS, CHILLI & GARLIC
SPATCHCOCK CHICKEN

Serves 4: prep: 10 minutes/marinate: 2 hours/cook: 1 hour 20 minutes

To spatchcock the chicken, take the whole chicken, place breast side down and with a pair of strong scissors remove the backbone by cutting from the tail end to the neck end either side of the backbone. Turn the chicken over and place the palm of your hand on the centre of the breast, pressing down to flatten out the chicken.

To prepare the marinade, mix all the marinade ingredients together and season with a large pinch of salt and freshly cracked black pepper. Place the chicken on a baking tray and pour over the marinade, rubbing it all over to ensure the chicken is fully covered on both sides. Marinate in the fridge covered with cling film for 2 hours.

To cook the chicken, pre-heat the oven to 170°C/325°F/gas mark 3. Roast the chicken for 45 minutes, basting in the juices every 15 minutes.

You can finish this recipe in two ways. Either remove the tin foil and cook for another 15-20 minutes basting in the juices occasionally until the core temperature, checked with a meat thermometer, has reached 75°c and the juices run clear.

Or, if finishing on the barbecue, remove the chicken from the juices in the tray and place on the barbecue, skin side up, for 5 minutes then turn over to colour the skin side for another 5 minutes, being careful not to burn it.

To serve, place on a board for sharing at the table and serve with a green salad and some sweet potato fries.

for the chicken
1.7kg free range chicken

for the marinade
3 tbsps olive oil
½ tsp dried chilli flakes
*3 cloves of garlic, peeled and
  finely chopped*
*1 red chilli, finely chopped,
  seeds included*
1 lemon, juice and zest
1 lime, juice and zest
40g honey
*2 tbsps fresh flat leaf parsley,
  roughly chopped*
sea salt & black pepper

COQ AU VIN

for the coq au vin
1 Norfolk chicken, cut into 10 pieces
(breasts cut in half, thighs,
drumsticks and wings with
the tips removed)
500ml red wine
25g butter
150g shallots, peeled
5 garlic cloves, peeled and
finely chopped
150g Woodall's Black Combe
air-dried ham, cut into strips
1 sprig of fresh thyme
350g button chestnut
mushrooms, washed
500ml fresh chicken stock
2 tbsps balsamic vinegar
sea salt & black pepper

for the ultimate mash
1kg Maris Piper potatoes, peeled and
chopped into evenly-sized pieces
90g clotted cream
100g unsalted butter
sea salt & white pepper

to serve
1 small bunch flat leaf parsley,
roughly chopped

Serves 4: prep: 20 minutes/marinate: 2 hours/cook: 45-55 minutes

To cook the coq au vin, marinate the chicken pieces in the red wine for 2 hours. Pre-heat the oven to 170°C /325°F/gas mark 3. Heat a thick -bottomed casserole dish on a medium to high heat, add the butter and the shallots and cook until just brown and caramelised. Add the garlic, ham and thyme and cook for 2-3 minutes.

Drain the red wine from the chicken and keep to one side. Add the mushrooms to the pan, then the red wine used for the marinade, chicken stock and vinegar and bring to a gentle simmer. Add the chicken pieces and bring the sauce back to the simmer. Once simmering, season with salt and freshly cracked black pepper and place the lid on the dish and put in the oven for about 40 minutes or until the chicken is tender and cooked through.

To make the ultimate mash, place the potatoes in a pan of cold water with a pinch of salt. Bring to the boil and simmer for 15-20 minutes until very tender. Whilst the potatoes are cooking heat up the cream and butter with a pinch of salt and pepper; when the butter has melted, stir in and remove from the heat. When the potato is cooked pass through a ricer into a bowl. Mix the butter and cream mixture through and again season to taste with salt and pepper.

To serve, sprinkle the chopped parsley on top of the coq au vin and serve in a bowl with some ultimate mashed potato.

CORN-FED WHOLE ROAST CHICKEN WITH PORK AND PANCETTA STUFFING

Serves 4: prep: 30 minutes/1hr 30 minutes – 2 hours

To make the stuffing, heat a frying pan on medium with the olive oil and lightly fry the pancetta and shallot until softened and starting to brown. When ready transfer to a bowl and add the ciabatta breadcrumbs, sausage meat, sage, lemon zest and season well with salt and freshly cracked black pepper. Mix this all together and put to one side whilst preparing the chicken.

To cook the chicken, pre-heat the oven to 180'C/350'F/gas mark 4. First make the garlic and herb butter by softening the butter in a microwave for 10 seconds. Be careful not to melt the butter. Add the chopped garlic, thyme, rosemary and lemon zest and mix well. Place the chopped carrot, celery and onion in a non-stick baking tray. Place the chicken on top of the chopped vegetables. Make two small slices in to the skin of the top of the chicken breasts so that you are able to pipe in the garlic and herb butter. When you have piped some of the mixture in, massage the butter down the breasts on the outside of the skin until evenly covered. If there is a little butter left over smooth over the outside of the chicken for extra flavour whilst cooking. Stuff the chicken cavity with the stuffing. Season the chicken well with salt and freshly cracked black pepper and pour over the olive oil ensuring the bird has been fully covered in olive oil. Place into the pre-heated oven and cook for 90 minutes basting occasionally with the natural juices. Check with your meat thermometer the thighs have reached a core temperature of 75'c, or that the juices run clear when making an incision on the meaty thigh. When cooked remove the chicken from the tray and place on a chopping board and cover with tin foil for 15 minutes before serving to allow the bird to rest.

To cook the chubby pigs, using scissors or a knife separate the linked Toulouse sausages. Now slightly squeeze in the middle of the sausage pushing the meat more to the ends of the casing to create two chubby cocktail sausages and twist the casing in the centre to separate them off. Cut the middle so you now have two mini chubby sausages. Continue with the remaining sausages. Wrap each chubby tightly with a rasher of streaky bacon. Pan fry the chubbys to brown before placing in the oven for 12-15 minutes to cook through.

To make the gravy, when you have taken the chicken out of the oven and placed it on a board to rest, carefully spoon off and discard the vegetables and any oil from the surface of the juices in the tray. Place the tray with the juices onto the stove top and on a low heat bring to a simmer. Whilst stirring gently pour in the flour until mixed in thoroughly. Add the chicken stock and white wine, mix, then pass through a sieve into a clean saucepan. Place the saucepan on a medium heat and bring to a simmer for 2 minutes to thicken.

To serve, carve the chicken and serve with the chubby pigs in blankets, gravy and a selection of seasonal vegetables and roast potatoes.

for the stuffing
1 tbsp olive oil
100g Woodall's pancetta, roughly chopped
100g shallot, peeled and finely chopped
120g ciabatta bread crumbs
200g sausage meat
1 tbsp fresh sage
1 lemon zest
sea salt & black pepper

for the chicken
1.6kg free range corn-fed whole chicken
130g butter
6 garlic cloves, peeled and finely chopped
1 tbsp fresh thyme leaves
1 tbsp fresh rosemary leaves
1 lemon zest
2 carrots, roughly chopped
2 sticks of celery, roughly chopped
1 large onion, peeled and roughly chopped
sea salt & black pepper
100ml olive oil

for the chubby pigs
1 pack Toulouse sausages
1 pack dry cured air-dried smoked streaky bacon

for the gravy
500ml Chicken Stock
50g Plain flour
100ml White wine

EAST MEETS WEST
DRY-CURED GAMMON JOINT
WITH PARSLEY SAUCE

for the gammon

1.5kg dry cured gammon joint
4 garlic cloves, finely chopped
1 red chilli, finely chopped,
  seeds removed
80g ginger, peeled and finely chopped
1 tbsp vegetable oil
80g dark soy sauce
100g light soy sauce
100g maple syrup
1 tsp cracked black pepper
1 tsp dried red pepper flakes

for the roast potatoes

900g Maris Piper potatoes,
  peeled and cut in half
3 tbsps duck fat
30g unsalted butter, roughly chopped
2 tsps Chinese five-spice
sea salt & black pepper

for the parsley sauce

200ml pork stock
350ml milk
40g unsalted butter
40g plain flour
60g finely chopped parsley
60ml double cream
1 lime juice and zest
sea salt & black pepper

for the green beans

200g French beans, topped and tailed
1 tbsp sesame oil
1 red chilli, thinly sliced,
  seeds removed
1 tsp sesame seeds

Serves 6: prep: 20 minutes/marinate: 24 hours/cook: 2 hours

To cook the gammon, prepare the marinade by lightly frying the chopped garlic, chilli and ginger in a pan with a little oil. Mix with the soy sauces, maple syrup, cracked black pepper and red pepper flakes. For best results place the gammon in a vacuum sealed bag with the marinade and leave for 24 hours; alternately marinade the joint in a sealed container and baste or turn the meat several times in the 24-hour marinating period. Once marinated pre-heat an oven to 180°C/350°F/ gas mark 4 and empty the gammon and its marinade into a non-stick baking dish and cover with tin foil. Bake for 60 minutes, basting every 20 minutes. After 60 minutes remove from the oven, turn the oven up to 220°C/425°F/gas mark 7, remove the tin foil, baste in the cooking liquor again then return to the oven for 15 minutes to colour the outside of the gammon. When cooked remove from the oven and test the temperature with your food meat thermometer to make sure the thickest part of the meat has reached 72°C. Let the meat rest for 15 minutes before serving.

To roast the potatoes, pre-heat an oven to 180°C/350°F/gas mark 4. Place the potatoes, duck fat, butter, Chinese five-spice in a high-sided baking tray and season with salt and freshly cracked black pepper. Mix the potatoes to completely cover in the fat and spices and place in the oven. Cook for 60 minutes, turning the potatoes over every 20 minutes until they are crisp and golden brown.

To make the parsley sauce, mix the stock and milk together in a saucepan and place on the heat to warm up, but do not boil. In another saucepan melt the butter and add the flour. Cook the flour and butter mixture for 90 seconds to remove the raw flour taste, then slowly add the hot milk and stock mixture, whisking to make the sauce smooth with no lumps. When all the milk and stock mixture is added bring to a simmer for 30 seconds. Remove from the heat and add the finely chopped parsley, cream, lime zest and juice and season to taste with salt and freshly cracked black pepper.

To cook the green beans, fill a medium-sized pan with water and bring to the boil on a high heat. Place the beans in the boiling water and cook for 90 seconds. Drain the beans through a sieve. Heat a frying pan on a high heat, add the sesame oil, chilli and green beans and lightly fry for another 90 seconds. Sprinkle with sesame seeds and remove from the heat and serve.

To serve, carve gammon slices and serve with the five-spice roasted potatoes, chilli and sesame green beans, and plenty of parsley sauce.

HAMPSHIRE RIB OF PORK

Serves 4-6 people: prep: 20 minutes/cook: 1 hour 30 minutes

To roast the pork, ensure the joint has a minimum of 12mm of fat to create the ultimate crackling. Place the joint on a wire rack and put in the kitchen sink. Boil a kettle of water and gently pour over to open up the scoring. Dry the rind thoroughly with kitchen paper. Place the joint on a wire rack over a baking tray, sprinkle with half the table salt and leave for 15 minutes at room temperature to draw out any remaining moisture.

Pre-heat the oven to 240°C/475°F/gas mark 9. Dry the rind again with kitchen paper. Brush sparingly with a little olive oil then sprinkle again with the remaining table salt. Place the tray into the oven and cook for 25-30 minutes until the crackling has started to pop and turn a golden brown. Turn the oven down to 170°C/325°F/gas mark 3 for the remainder of the roasting time; about another 30-40 minutes. Check the core temperature of the pork has reached 70°C with your meat thermometer. Allow the meat to rest for 15 minutes before carving the joint between the bones.

To make the gravy, pre-heat the oven to 200°C/400°F/gas mark 6. Put half the vegetables and all of the bones, evenly mixed, in two roasting trays and coat with a little vegetable oil. Roast in the oven for 20 minutes until caramelised. Transfer everything to a saucepan, add the thyme, garlic, bay leaf, rosemary, peppercorns and fennel seeds, and cover with cold water. Bring to a simmer and cook for 4 hours, reducing by two-thirds, skimming every half an hour to remove any impurities and fat on top of the stock.

In a separate saucepan bring the butter to a foam and lightly colour the pork trimmings and other half of the vegetables. Once everything is evenly caramelised, add the bacon lardons and cider, and simmer to reduce by half. Strain the first batch of stock into the saucepan with the reduced cider and continue to reduce by two-thirds. Finally thicken to the desired consistency using the cornflour and water mixture whilst stiring, cook out the sauce for 2 minutes. Season with fine salt to taste before straining through a fine sieve.

To make the apple ketchup, place the apple into a saucepan with the cider vinegar, sugar, vanilla pod and seeds and the butter. Cook over a low heat, stirring occasionally to break down the apple to a purée, this should take around 10-12 minutes. Pass through a sieve or blend with a stick blender to achieve a smooth apple ketchup.

To make ultimate mash, place the potatoes in a pan of water with a pinch of salt. Bring to the boil, simmer for 15-20 minutes until tender. Whilst the potatoes are cooking heat up the cream and butter with a pinch of salt and pepper. When the butter has melted, stir in and remove from the heat. When the potato is cooked pass through a ricer into a bowl. Mix the butter and cream mixture through and again season to taste with salt and pepper.

To serve, place the pork in the centre of the table for a roast dinner, and serve with ultimate mash, apple ketchup and some seasonal vegetables.

for the pork
2kg Hampshire pork rib joint,
   minimum 12mm fat depth, rind-on
   and diamond-scored
20ml olive oil
4 tbsps table salt

for the gravy
375g carrots, roughly chopped
375g onion, roughly chopped
375g leeks, roughly chopped
375g celery, roughly chopped
1kg pork bones, small pieces
30ml vegetable oil
1 tbsp fresh thyme leaves
6 garlic cloves, peeled
1 bay leaf
1 rosemary sprig
5 black peppercorns
1 tsp fennel seeds
2l water
50g butter
500g pork trimmings, roughly diced
125g smoked bacon lardons
250ml cider
2 tbsps cornflour, mixed with
   3 tbsps of water

for the apple ketchup
190g Bramley apple, peeled and diced
20ml cider vinegar
25g sugar
1 vanilla pod, cut in half
   and seeds removed
20g unsalted butter

for ultimate mash
1kg Maris Piper potatoes, peeled and
   chopped into evenly-sized pieces
90g clotted cream
100g unsalted butter
sea salt & white pepper

HEAP'S BANGERS AND MASH WITH BLACK KALE AND CRISPY SHALLOTS

for the sausages

60g horseradish sauce
20g double cream
24 rashers of dry-cured
air-dried streaky bacon
2 tbsps vegetable oil
12 thick premium pork sausages

for the sauce smitaine

25g unsalted butter
1 banana shallot, finely chopped
30ml white wine
30ml white wine vinegar
400ml single cream
25g gherkins, finely shredded

for the purple mash

600g purple sweet potatoes,
peeled and evenly chopped
1 tsp salt
100g butter
large pinch of salt and cracked black
pepper for finishing

for the kale

120g black kale
60g unsalted butter
sea salt & black pepper

for the crispy shallots

3 banana shallots, peeled and sliced
into thin rings
3 tbsps milk
100g plain flour, seasoned with salt
and cracked black pepper
200ml vegetable oil

Serves 4: prep: 20 minutes/cook: 35-45 minutes

To cook the sausages, pre-heat the oven to 200°C/400°F/gas mark 6. Mix the horseradish sauce and cream together and using a pastry brush coat each sausage with the mix, then wrap each one tightly with 2 rashers of slightly overlapped streaky bacon. Heat the vegetable oil in a frying pan over a medium to high heat then add the bacon-wrapped sausages and cook until the bacon is golden brown on all sides. Place the sausages on a non-stick tray and bake in the pre-heated oven for 8-10 minutes until the temperature in the middle of the sausages reaches 70°C, use a meat thermometer to check.

To make the sauce smitaine, melt the butter in a thick-bottomed saucepan over a low to medium heat and cook the shallots slowly without colouring them. Add the wine and vinegar and reduce the volume by a half. Add the cream and reduce by a third until the consistency is thick enough to coat the sausages. Add the gherkins and season to taste, then serve.

To make the purple mash, add the sweet potatoes to a large saucepan and cover with cold water. Bring the pan to the boil and then add the salt. Reduce the heat to a simmer for around 20 minutes until soft. Drain off the water, add the butter and seasoning and mash to a smooth purée.

To cook the kale, boil some salted water in a saucepan. Cut away any heavy stalks from the leaves. Blanch the leaves until you can fold them without snapping. Drain and add the butter to melt over the kale leaves, season with salt and freshly cracked black pepper.

To cook the crispy shallots, soak the shallot rings in the milk for 5 minutes. Drain then toss in seasoned flour to coat. Shallow-fry in hot oil until golden and crispy. Drain on kitchen paper and sprinkle with a little salt.

To serve, place some purple mash on the centre of the plate and gently spread across. Scatter some black kale over the mash and place two sausages on top. Finish with the shallot rings and drizzle with sauce smitaine.

HOG ROAST WITH
APPLE KETCHUP

Serves 4: prep: 40 minutes/cook: 3 hours

To make the stuffing, in a frying pan over a medium heat fry the
shallots in a little oil for 2 minutes until softened. Empty the shallots into
a mixing bowl and allow to cool for 10 minutes. Place the ciabatta in a food
processor and blend into breadcrumbs. Add the sausage meat, sage and
lemon zest to the bowl with the shallots, season with a large pinch of salt
and freshly cracked black pepper and mix together to a firm stuffing.

To roast the pork, open up the joint and evenly place the stuffing
across the length of the joint. Close the joint over the stuffing and tie with
butcher's string at 1-inch intervals. Place the joint on a wire rack and place
in the sink. Pre-heat the oven to 240°C/475°F/gas mark 9. Boil a kettle of
water and pour over the joint to open up the scoring on the rind. Pat dry
with kitchen towel to remove as much moisture as possible. Rub the rind
with olive oil, just enough to coat it so the seasoning sticks. Season the rind
evenly with salt. Place in the pre-heated oven and cook for 30 minutes.
Once done, reduce the temperature to 180°c/350°F/gas mark 4 and cook
for 2-2½ hours until the core temperature in the thickest part of the joint
reaches 70°C measured on a meat thermometer. When cooked remove
from the oven and allow to rest for 20 minutes before serving.

To make the apple ketchup, place the apple into a saucepan with
the cider vinegar, sugar, vanilla pod and seeds and the butter. Cook over
a low heat, stirring occasionally to break down the apple to a purée, this
should take 10-12 minutes. Pass through a sieve or blend with a stick
blender to achieve a smooth apple ketchup.

To serve, this pork is best served street food style, sliced up and served
in buttered crusty sour dough rolls with plenty of apple ketchup, crackling
and stuffing or alternatively as the centre piece for an awesome Sunday
roast dinner.

for the stuffing
*150g shallots, peeled and
    finely chopped*
1 tbsp vegetable oil
200g ciabatta
200g sausage meat
20g fresh sage, finely chopped
1 lemon zest
sea salt & black pepper

for the pork
*2kg rind-on, diamond-scored
    pork shoulder neck fillet,
    butchered to take stuffing*
1 tbsp of olive oil
4 tbsps table salt

for the apple ketchup
190g Bramley apple, peeled and diced
20ml cider vinegar
25g sugar
*1 vanilla pod, cut in half
    and seeds removed*
20g unsalted butter

LOUISIANA CREOLE PORK STEAK WITH DIRTY RICE AND LIME CRÈME FRAICHE

for the dirty rice

200g basmati rice
250ml water
sea salt
1 medium white onion, finely chopped
1 tbsp vegetable oil
3 garlic cloves, peeled and
  finely chopped
400g pork mince (5% fat)
½ tsp black pepper
¼ tsp cayenne pepper
1 tbsp fresh thyme leaves,
  stalks removed
1 celery stick, finely diced
2 green peppers, diced
20g fresh flat leaf parsley,
  roughly chopped

for the lime crème fraiche

1 lime, juice and zest
150g crème fraiche
sea salt & black pepper

for the creole pork

4 x 150g thin pork leg steaks
25g Maldon sea salt
10g dried garlic granules
10g smoked paprika
½ tsp dried oregano
¼ tsp cayenne pepper
½ tsp dried thyme
½ tsp cracked black pepper
½ tsp black onion seeds

Serves 4: prep: 20 minutes/cook: 30 minutes

To make the dirty rice, place the rice, water and a large pinch of salt in a pan and stir well together. Bring the rice to the boil, place the lid on the pan and turn off the heat. Leave for 20 minutes to soak up the liquid then fluff up with a fork.

In a large frying pan over a medium heat, fry the onion and garlic in a little vegetable oil until starting to colour. Add the pork mince and fry, mixing to break up the meat. When starting to brown, add the black pepper, cayenne and fresh thyme and mix well. Add the celery and diced green pepper and cook for another two minutes. Finally, mix in the parsley. Add the rice to the pan and mix through.

To make the lime crème fraiche, mix the lime juice and zest with the crème fraiche and season with a large pinch of salt and freshly cracked black pepper.

To cook the pork, mix together all the spices and sprinkle over both sides of the pork leg steaks. Heat a griddle pan over a high heat until smoking hot and add a little vegetable oil. Griddle the steaks for around 45 seconds on each side. Remove from the heat and leave to rest on a warm plate for 2 minutes before serving.

To serve, place some dirty rice in a bowl, top with the pork steaks and drizzle with the lime crème fraiche.

MARINATED SLOW-COOKED GAMMON SHANK WITH BUBBLE AND SQUEAK

Serves 4: prep: 20 minutes/marinate: 4 days/
sous vide 5 hours 30 minutes/cook: 35-40 minutes

To cure the gammon, mix the dry curing ingredients well together
and rub into the meat. Place in a sealable plastic container and keep in
the fridge for 3-4 days. Remove, rinse in cold water and they're ready for
marinating before cooking.

To cook the shanks, preset your sous vide machine to 90°C.
Place the washed gammons carefully in a vacuum sealing bag with the
juniper berries and cinnamon stick (don't overcrowd the bag: you don't
want the shanks sticking together when cooking). Warm the honey in
a microwave for 20 seconds then mix 120g honey and ground cloves
together in a bowl and pour into the bag with the shanks. Vacuum seal
the bag. Place the bag in the sous vide machine for 5 hours 30 minutes.

When cooked the shanks can be rapid-chilled in the bag (submerge in
icy water to reduce the temperature quickly) before storing in the fridge.
When ready to cook, pre-heat the oven to 200°C, remove the meat from
the bag gently so it doesn't fall off the bone, place on a non-stick
baking tray coated in olive oil and drizzle with the rest of the honey.
Bake in the oven for 15 minutes, basting with the honey mixture to
caramelise the outer crust of the shanks.

To cook the shanks (without a sous vide machine), pre-heat the oven
to 140°C/275°F/gas mark 4. In a high-sided baking tray add the shanks,
juniper berries, cinnamon stick, honey, ground clove and 250ml of cold
water. Cover with tin foil and place in the oven for 2½ hours, removing
from the oven and basting in the juices every 30 minutes. After 2½ hours
remove the tray from the oven and discard the tin foil. Increase the heat
to 180°C/350°F/gas mark 4 and cook for 30-35 minutes basting halfway
through until golden brown and caramelized.

To make the bubble and squeak, parboil the potatoes so they still have
a little bite. In a frying pan over a medium heat pan-fry the onion, carrot
and lardons in a little sunflower oil until starting to brown. Add the garlic,
chilli, crumbled stock cube and the sprouts. Cook for another 2 minutes,
stirring occasionally. Add the potatoes and mix through. Turn the heat to
high to create a crust on the bubble and squeak before turning over with
a wooden spoon. Cook for another 8-10 minutes stirring occasionally to
get some golden crust running throughout the bubble. Add the chopped
parsley and season with salt and freshly cracked black pepper to taste.

for the dry cure

*4 'spoon bone' Hampshire pork
  shanks trimmed (about 350g each)*
70g salt
30g sugar
1tsp saltpetre

for the shanks

10 juniper berries
1 cinnamon stick
200g honey
1 large pinch of ground cloves
80ml olive oil

for the bubble and squeak

*600g Maris Piper potatoes, skin on
  and diced evenly*
1 large onion, roughly chopped
2 medium carrots, coarsely grated
100g unsmoked bacon lardons
1 tbsp sunflower oil
2 garlic cloves, finely chopped
1 red chilli, finely chopped
1 chicken stock cube
*120g Brussels sprouts, tops removed
  and cut into quarters*
sea salt & black pepper
*1 small bunch fresh parsley,
  roughly chopped*

'NDUJA-STUFFED CHICKEN WITH WOODALL'S PANCETTA AND FENNEL-ROASTED NEW POTATOES

for the chicken
4 x 170g skinless chicken breasts
120g smoked cheddar cheese, cut into
    4 rectangular pieces
120g of 'nduja
sea salt & black pepper
1 tsp dried chives
3 packs Woodall's smoked pancetta

for the potatoes
600g Charlotte potatoes
1 bulb of fennel, thick sliced
6 cloves garlic, skin-on
8 sprigs of fresh thyme
5 sprigs of fresh rosemary
80ml extra virgin olive oil
sea salt & black pepper

for the salsa verde
1 bunch parsley, stalks included
1 bunch basil, stalks included
2 lemons, juiced
1 clove garlic, peeled
½ red chilli, seeds and stalk removed
4 anchovy fillets
sea salt & black pepper

to serve
2 red chillies, finely sliced
1 small bunch of fresh chives,
    cut into 6cm batons

Serves 4: prep: 20 minutes/cook: 30-40 minutes

To prepare the chicken, cut an incision on the bottom side of each chicken breast; don't cut all the way through. Stuff the breast with a rectangle of smoked cheese and a roughly equal quantity of 'nduja. Season with a pinch of salt and freshly cracked black pepper and sprinkle with some dried chives. Close the chicken breasts and place the open side face down onto a tray.

Lay out 6 slices of pancetta on greaseproof paper with a gap of 10mm between each rasher. Weave another 6 rashers through them to create a lattice square. Repeat the process 3 more times so you have 4 woven lattice squares.

Place the chicken breasts on top of the pancetta mats and with the aid of the baking paper fold the pancetta around the breast to form an oval-shaped parcel. Remove from the baking paper and place on a baking tray with the join of the pancetta on the bottom.

To make the potatoes, pre-heat the oven to 200°C/400°F/gas mark 6. Slice the Charlotte potatoes in half (try to get them evenly-sized) and place in a baking tray. Add the sliced fennel and mix with the potatoes. Mix in the skin-on garlic cloves, thyme sprigs, rosemary sprigs, olive oil and season with a large pinch of salt and freshly cracked black pepper and place in the pre-heated oven for 45 minutes, turning occasionally.

To cook the chicken, pre-heat the oven to 200°C/400°F/gas mark 6. Bake for 25-30 minutes until the core temperature has reached 75°C measured on a meat thermometer. Remove from the oven and allow to rest on a warm plate. Slice the chicken and spoon on the juices that have formed while cooking.

For the salsa verde dressing, place all the ingredients in a food blender, season with salt and freshly cracked black pepper and blend to a smooth sauce.

To serve, slice the chicken in 2cm thick slices and serve on a plate with the fennel-roasted new potatoes and a generous spoonful of salsa verde. Scatter with sliced chillies and garnish with chives.

ROSEMARY-ROASTED HAMPSHIRE PORK LOIN

Serves 4: prep: 25 minutes/cook: 65-75 minutes

To cook the pork, pre-heat the oven to 245°C/475°F/gas mark 9. Mix the rosemary with the sea salt. Place the loin rind side down on a chopping board. Slice into the eye of the loin meat from the side of the joint and slice it open without slicing all the way through so it resembles an open book. Sprinkle evenly with three-quarters of the rosemary salt and roll the loin back up to its original shape. Tie firmly with string to hold together. Place the joint on a wire rack and place in a sink, and then pour boiling water over the rind. Dry off the rind with paper towel and drizzle the rind with the olive oil and finish with the remaining rosemary salt. Place onto a tray and put into the pre-heated oven for 35 minutes, then turn down to 220°C/425°F/gas mark 7 for a further 30 minutes.

To make the Chantenay carrots, place the carrots in a saucepan of cold water with a large pinch of salt and freshly cracked black pepper. Bring to the boil and then simmer for 8-10 minutes so they still have some bite. Drain. Add the butter and sugar to the pan and put on a medium heat and stir. Leave the carrots long enough to colour before stirring.

To make ultimate mash, place the potatoes in a pan of water with a pinch of salt. Bring to the boil, simmer for 15-20 minutes until tender. Whilst the potatoes are cooking heat up the cream and butter with a pinch of salt and pepper. When the butter has melted, stir in and remove from the heat. When the potato is cooked pass through a ricer into a bowl. Mix the butter and cream mixture through and again season to taste with salt and pepper.

To make the red wine jus, heat a saucepan on a medium heat and fry the shallots in olive oil until lightly caramelised. Stir in the garlic and thyme. Pour in the vinegar, red wine and chicken stock, and reduce by just over half, remove from the heat and sieve into a clean pan. Just before serving heat the sauce to the boil and add the butter, stirring all the time until incorporated, and season with salt and freshly cracked black pepper.

To make the maple apple sauce, place the chopped apple into a pan with 150ml of water and a large pinch of salt. Bring to the boil and on a low to medium heat continue to cook until the apple cooks enough to mash into a nice sauce. To finish, add 100ml of Canadian maple syrup and season with freshly cracked black pepper to taste.

To caramelise the apples, pre-heat an over to 180°C/350°F/gas mark 4. In a bowl coat the apples in the maple syrup and season with salt and freshly cracked black pepper, toss the apples to ensure they are evenly coated. Place on a non-stick tray and put in the oven for 15-20 minutes until the apples caramelise. Remove from the oven and serve.

To serve, when the loin has cooked remove from the oven and set aside to rest for 15 minutes. Cut the string and remove the crackling, then set to one side. Carve the loin thinly and serve with the maple apple sauce, break up the crackling with a knife and serve with the maple apple sauce, mash, carrots, some steamed stem broccoli, caramelised apples and red wine jus.

for the pork
1kg rind-on Hampshire pork loin
  (rind scored and patted dry)
1 bunch rosemary, stalks removed,
  finely chopped
1 tbsp sea salt flakes
olive oil

for the Chantenay carrots
400g Chantenay carrots, peeled
sea salt & black pepper
80g demerara sugar
40g unsalted butter

for ultimate mash
1kg Maris Piper potatoes, peeled and
  chopped into evenly-sized pieces
90g clotted cream
100g unsalted butter
sea salt & white pepper

for the red wine jus
125g shallot, finely chopped
2 tbsps olive oil
1 garlic clove, finely chopped
1 sprig thyme, leaves only
3 tbsps balsamic vinegar
125ml red wine
425ml chicken stock
25g butter
sea salt & black pepper

for the maple apple sauce
4 large Bramley apples, peeled,
  cored and evenly chopped
100ml Canadian maple syrup
sea salt & black pepper

for the caramelised apples
2 Pink Lady apples, cored
  and quartered
50ml maple syrup
sea salt & black pepper

SLOW-COOKED PIGS' CHEEKS IN RED WINE JUS

for the pigs' cheeks
4 pigs' cheeks, fully trimmed
sea salt & black pepper
1 banana shallot, finely chopped
3 sprigs of thyme, leaves only
60ml red wine

for the red wine jus
2 tbsps olive oil
125g shallots, finely chopped
1 garlic clove, finely chopped
1 sprig thyme, leaves only
3 tbsps balsamic vinegar
125ml red wine
all of the liquor from the slow
* cooking of the pigs' cheeks*
125ml chicken stock
25g butter
sea salt & black pepper

for ultimate mash
1kg maris piper potatoes, peeled and
* chopped into evenly-sized pieces*
90g clotted cream
100g unsalted butter
sea salt & black pepper

for the caramelised carrots
400g Chantanay carrots, peeled
sea salt & black pepper
80g demerara sugar
40g unsalted butter

for the crispy pancetta
100g of sliced smoked
* pancetta rashers*

Serves 4: prep: 20 minutes/sous vide: 7 hours/cook: 30-35 minutes

To make the pigs' cheeks (this can only be done sous vide), fill your sous vide machine with water and set at 85°C. Season the pigs' cheeks with a large pinch of salt and freshly cracked black pepper. Pan-fry the cheeks to colour on both sides and set them aside on a tray for later. In the same pan, fry the banana shallot and thyme until tender and only lightly coloured, add the red wine and reduce by a third. Add the cheeks and the reduced red wine mixture to a sous vide bag and seal with a vacuum sealer. Sous vide the cheeks for 7 hours at 85°C.

To make the red wine jus, heat a saucepan on a medium heat and fry the shallots in oilve oil until lightly caramelised. Stir in the garlic and thyme. Pour in the vinegar and reduce, followed by the red wine and liquor taken from the bag of cooked pigs' cheeks, and reduce again. Next add the chicken stock and reduce by two-thirds, remove from the heat and sieve into a clean pan. Just before serving heat the sauce to the boil and add the butter, stirring all the time until incorporated, and season with salt and freshly cracked black pepper.

To make ultimate mash, place the potatoes in a pan of cold water with a pinch of salt. Bring to the boil and simmer for 15-20 minutes until very tender. Whilst the potatoes are cooking heat up the cream and butter with a pinch of salt and freshly cracked black pepper; when the butter has melted, stir in and remove from the heat. For the best results, when the potato is cooked, pass through a ricer into a bowl. Mix the butter and cream mixture through and again season to taste with salt and pepper.

To make the Chantenay carrots, place the carrots in a saucepan of cold water with a large pinch of salt and freshly cracked black pepper. Bring to the boil and then simmer for 8-10 minutes so they still have some bite. Drain. Add the butter and demerara sugar to the pan and put back on a medium to high heat and stir. Leave the carrots long enough to colour before stirring.

To make the crispy pancetta, place a piece of greaseproof paper on a baking tray and lay the pancetta slices on top, slightly separated. Place another sheet of greaseproof paper on top, followed by another baking tray to keep the bacon flat and help the crisping up during cooking. Bake in the oven at 190°C/375°F/gas mark 5 for approximately 8-10 minutes or until crispy.

To serve, spoon the mash into the centre of each plate, add the carrots, pigs' cheeks and pancetta, pour over the red wine jus and garnish with fresh thyme leaves.

SLOW-ROASTED SOY AND BALSAMIC GLAZED HAMPSHIRE PORK BELLY WITH SAUTÉED PAK-CHOI

Serves 4: prep: 20 minutes/marinate: 24 hours/cook: 2 hours

To marinade the belly, in a bowl mix together the soy, balsamic, honey, chilli and garlic. Place the belly in a deep oven tray and fully coat with the marinade. Cover the tray and refrigerate for 24 hours, turning the meat over after 12 hours to allow the flavours to soak in.

To cook the belly, pre-heat the oven to 140°C/275°F/gas mark 1. Remove the tray from the fridge and cover with tin foil, ensuring that it doesn't touch the rind of the belly during cooking or it will stick to the foil. Cook for 2 hours, checking occasionally that the marinade hasn't dried out: if it's nearly dry, add a little water so that it doesn't burn. Once the pork belly has become sticky and the meat tender, remove from the oven and allow to rest on a warm plate. If the juices are quite thick in the bottom of the tray you are ready to serve however; if the juices from the pork are quite thin, pour them into a pan and reduce on a low heat to a double cream-like consistency to create the balsamic glaze.

To sauté the pak choi, heat a wok or frying pan on a medium heat. Once hot add the sesame oil and mushrooms and cook for 1 minute, stirring the mushrooms halfway through. Add the garlic and ginger, mix in and cook for another minute, then add the pak choi, a splash of water and the fish sauce. Cook for 2 minutes until the pak choi is cooked but still crunchy.

To serve, slice the belly pork and place in a bowl with the sautéed pak choi and mushrooms and drizzle with the balsamic glaze.

for the belly
700g Hampshire rind-on
   pork belly piece
150ml soy sauce
8 tbsps balsamic vinegar
3 tbsps honey
1 tsp chilli flakes
1 tsp garlic, finely chopped

for the sautéed pak choi
1 tbsp sesame oil
100g shitake mushrooms,
   sliced into quarters
1 tsp garlic, finely chopped
½ tsp ginger, finely chopped
4 pak choi, sliced into quarters
1 tbsp fish sauce

SMOKED GARLIC BUTTER CHICKEN KIEV

for the chicken Kiev

4 x 160g chicken breasts, skin and
*   bone off, inner fillet remaining*
8 cloves smoked garlic, finely chopped
20g chives, finely chopped
100g unsalted butter, softened
*   (but not melted!)*
smoked sea salt
100g plain flour
10g smoked paprika
2 eggs
200g panko breadcrumbs

for the American slaw

1 sweetcorn on the cob
1 tbsp corn oil
sea salt & black pepper
1 small green cabbage
4 spring onions
20g parsley
2 medium carrots
50ml cider vinegar
120g full fat mayonnaise
1 tsp black onion seeds

Serves 4: prep: 20 minutes/cook: 20-25 minutes

To make the Kievs, put the smoked garlic and chives into a bowl. Add the softened butter and a large pinch of smoked sea salt and mix to a smooth paste for piping in a piping bag. Place the chicken breasts on a sturdy chopping board and remove just one of the inner fillets to use later. Using a sharp filleting knife create a deep pocket for the garlic butter by slicing from the thick end of the breast well into it. Using a piping bag fill the pocket with the smoked garlic and chive butter. Cut the reserved inner fillet into four equal-sized pieces and use it to plug the holes.

Pre-heat the oven to 180°C/350°F/gas mark 4. In three separate dishes prepare the seasoned flour with smoked paprika, whisked whole eggs and panko breadcrumbs. Place the chicken breasts in the seasoned flour ensuring the breast is fully covered. Do the same with the egg and finally with the breadcrumbs; make sure there are no gaps in the crust. In a frying pan heat a generous amount of sunflower oil until very hot and pan-fry the Kievs for 90 seconds on each side to create a golden crust. Place onto a non-stick baking tray and bake in the oven for 15-20 minutes.

To make the slaw, drizzle the corn with the corn oil, season with a pinch of salt and freshly cracked black pepper and griddle on a high heat until the corn appears almost burnt. Slice the kernels from the cob and leave to cool. Finely slice the cabbage (if you have a mandoline use this to achieve consistency). Slice the spring onion, chop the parsley and peel and grate the carrot. Mix all the chopped vegetables and herbs together and add the cider vinegar. Finally add the mayonnaise and onion seeds, mix well and season to taste.

To serve, place the chicken Kievs straight from the oven on warmed plates, and add a good serving of slaw.

FULL MONTY ONE-PAN BREAKFAST WITH JACK SCAIFE'S DRY-CURE BACON AND HEAP'S CHIPOLATAS

Serves 4: prep: 10 minutes/cook: 30 minutes

To fry the chipolatas, pre-heat 1 tablespoon of vegetable oil in a large frying pan on a medium heat and pan-fry the sausages until golden brown, turning every 2-3 minutes. The sausages will take around 12 minutes to cook. Once cooked remove the sausages to a plate lined with kitchen towel to soak up any excess fat.

To cook the bacon, heat the grill to high. Place the rashers slightly apart on a grill tray and cook under the grill for 2-3 minutes until the bacon has curled and the fat is golden brown; turn over and cook for another 90 seconds. Remove the bacon to the plate with the sausages.

To cook the vegetables, return the pan to the heat and turn it up to high. Add the remaining tablespoon of vegetable oil and add the mushrooms and asparagus and fry for 2 minutes, turning occasionally. Add the spinach and cook until it has wilted. Remove the vegetables to a sieve to drain any excess water.

To cook the tomatoes, place the tomatoes on the grill tray used for the bacon and drizzle with the olive oil and season with salt and freshly cracked black pepper. Place under the grill for 2 minutes until the skin is starting to pop.

To finish, place the sausages back into the pan and warm on a high heat for 60 seconds, return the bacon to the pan, crack in the eggs and turn the heat down to low. Spoon the vegetables back into the pan around the eggs followed by the baked beans and tomatoes. Cook on the low heat for 3-4 minutes until the eggs are cooked but yolk is still slightly runny.

for the breakfast
2 tbsps vegetable oil
1 pack of premium pork chipolatas, links cut
1 pack of smoked or unsmoked dry cured air-dried back bacon
250g small portabello mushrooms
150g asparagus, trimmed
500g spinach, washed and dried
260g cherry tomatoes
1 tbsp olive oil
sea salt & black pepper
4 medium free range eggs
200g Heinz baked beans

SMALL PLATES

90 — 119

CHARCUTERIE
— Colin Woodall, Woodall's

The Woodall's story, one of necessity being the mother of invention, begins with Hannah Woodall. In 1828 in Waberthwaite, Cumbria, Hannah lost her husband and needed a way to make ends meet and care for her family. She acquired her knowledge and butchery skills through helping other families slaughter and cure their pigs and used old family curing recipes to start a business; these recipes have continued to be handed down through the family to this day.

Colin Woodall is the eighth generation since Hannah and under his stewardship has seen the business grow to new heights.

"It's easy to forget where things come from," he says. "Back in the early days of our family business most families kept pigs. They were much bigger animals in those days. They were Cumberland pigs, which are now extinct, and were much fatter than modern breeds.

"They used every part of the animal and they had to. It was precious food back then and in the north the winters were long. So, to be expert in using up all those parts of the animal was a real asset. Typically the rear legs were turned into hams – and some of these hams could be enormous – and the belly and forelegs were used for bacon and sausage; even the sausage casings would have come from the pig.

"Slowly but surely the family started to produce ham, bacon and sausages for sale using the same old recipes. The quality of the products meant that they adorned some of the finest menus: our Cumberland ham was part of the buffet on the Titanic, for example, and later our sausages were eaten on Concorde. It's something I'm very proud of.

"Down the generations new products have been added into the range, from Cumberland sausages inspired by spices arriving from the new world into Whitehaven port, to fully air-dried charcuterie inspired by curing methods from the past.

"People have heard of the term charcuterie and associate it solely with products from the continent such as Parma ham and chorizo. The reality is that charcuterie, being air-dried, cured meats, has been produced here for centuries; the method of production is a method used to preserve meats. What happened was that the pigs were slaughtered and cured in the autumn. The hams, bacon and thick sausages were then hung in attics and barns to start to dry out.

"The perception is that charcuterie is a separate process but that's not the case. The charcuterie was the consequence and the only thing that defined it was the age of the cure. So, it was perfectly natural for us to bring back our old cures and methods and make British charcuterie."

IT'S A PRODUCT WITH A
GREAT FAMILY HERITAGE,
TIES IN WITH OUR FAMILY
TRADITIONS AND IS
UNIQUELY BRITISH.
WE MAKE BRITISH
CHARCUTERIE.
WE DON'T SIMPLY
MAKE CHARCUTERIE
IN BRITAIN.

1815

Black Combe

Batch 116

Logs 6124-6183

Delivery date:

09/03/2017

Pallet Nr.

1661086

Sugna w/c

23/04/17

WOODALL'S BRITISH CHARCUTERIE PLATTER WITH CUMBERLAND RING AND CRACKLING STRAWS

for the crackling straws
1kg pork loin rind
4 tbsps table salt

for the pickled red onions
100ml cider vinegar
1 orange juice and zest
½ tsp mustard seeds
½ tsp fennel seeds
6 black peppercorns
2 medium red onions,
*   peeled and sliced*

for the pancetta crisps
100g Woodall's pancetta

for the Cumberland ring
2 tbsps vegetable oil
1 x Woodall's 94% Cumberland ring

to serve
1 sourdough loaf, sliced into
*   thick slices*
2 tbsp olive oil
70g Woodall's Norfolk
*   Mustard Salami*
70g Woodall's Royale Ham
200g mature cheddar cheese,
*   cut into wedges*
4 tbsps English mustard
160g lamb's lettuce, washed and dried

Serves 4: prep: 30 minutes/cook: 45-55 minutes

To make the crackling straws, pre-heat an oven to 240°C/475°F/gas mark 9. Place the pork, rind side down, on a chopping board. Using a very sharp knife cut 1cm wide strips of rind and place them on a non-stick baking tray, rind side up. Sprinkle with the table salt. Place in the oven for 25-35 minutes until the rind is crisp and golden brown. Transfer to another tray lined with kitchen towel to soak up any excess fat.

To pickle the onions, place the cider vinegar, orange juice and zest, mustard seeds, fennel seeds and black peppercorns in a saucepan. Bring to the boil on a medium heat to allow the spices to infuse into the liquid. Once boiled remove from the heat and put the sliced onions into the liquor, ensuring they are fully covered. Place a lid on the pan and leave for 1 hour at room temperature to pickle.

To make the pancetta crisps, line a baking sheet with non-stick greaseproof paper and place the strips of pancetta on the tray, spaced apart. Place another sheet of non-stick greaseproof paper on top followed by another baking tray to keep the pancetta flat while cooking. Using the same pre-heated oven at 240°C/475°F/gas mark 9, bake for 8-10 minutes until crisp and golden brown. Transfer the pancetta crisps to another tray lined with kitchen towel to soak off any excess fat.

To cook the Cumberland ring, pre-heat an oven to 180°C/350°F/gas mark 4. Place a griddle pan over a medium heat. Coat the ring with the vegetable oil. Place the Cumberland ring in the hot pan and cook for 4 minutes on each side without moving the sausage so you get good griddle marks. Put the ring on a non-stick tray and place in the oven for 10-12 minutes until cooked through and the skins are crisp and golden brown.

To serve, pre-heat an oven to 180°C/350°F/gas mark 4. Place the sourdough slices on a baking tray and drizzle with the olive oil. Place the tray in the oven to lightly toast the bread for 3 minutes. Place the salamis, ham and cheese on a board, cover with cling film and leave to come to room temperature for 10 minutes; this allows the flavours to develop. Add the rest of the components to the board and serve.

WOODALL'S BLACK COMBE
AIR-DRIED HAM-WRAPPED PORK
FILLET WITH CALVADOS JUS

Serves 4: prep: 20 minutes/cook: 25-30 minutes

To cook the pork, on a board lay out the Black Combe air-dried ham, overlapping the edges a bit so that it is the same length as your piece of pork. Place the pork in the middle of the ham. Mix all the herbs together and rub all over the pork; don't worry if some falls off. Pull up the sides of the ham to wrap the pork tightly.

Place a large lidded casserole pan that easily fits the pork over a medium heat and add the olive oil. When it's hot, brown the pork on each side for a minute or so until the ham is golden. Be very careful when turning it over to avoid the ham slipping off the pork fillet. Season with salt and freshly cracked black pepper, pour over the stock and apple juice and place the lid on top. Place in the oven for 20 minutes, removing the lid or foil for the last 10 minutes. Remove from the oven and pour off the juices into a bowl and reserve, cover the pork again and leave to rest while you prepare the mash and sauce.

To make ultimate mash, place the potatoes in a pan of cold water with a pinch of salt. Bring to the boil and simmer for 15-20 minutes until very tender. Whilst the potatoes are cooking heat up the cream and butter with a pinch of salt and pepper; when the butter has melted, stir in and remove from the heat. For the best results, when the potato is cooked pass through a ricer into a bowl. Mix the butter and cream mixture through and again season to taste with salt and pepper.

To make the sauce, in a frying pan add the butter and gently fry the shallot and apple wedges for 2 minutes on a medium heat. Add the Calvados and cook for 1 minute then add the stock and reserved cooking juices. Reduce slightly for 3-4 minute, add the whipping cream, the vinegar and a good pinch of salt and cracked black pepper. If you want a thicker sauce you can thicken slightly with a small amount of the cornflour mixed with water.

To serve, slice the pork into 1cm thick slices and arrange on a large warmed serving plate with the ultimate mashed potatoes and the apple and Calvados sauce.

for the pork
8 slices of Woodall's Black Combe air-dried ham
500g pork tenderloin
2 tbsps fresh parsley, finely chopped
½ tbsp fresh thyme, finely chopped
½ tbsp fresh sage, finely chopped
½ tbsp fresh rosemary, roughly chopped
2 tbsps olive oil
sea salt & black pepper
100ml chicken stock
100ml of good cloudy apple juice

for ultimate mash
1kg Maris Piper potatoes, peeled and chopped into evenly-sized pieces
90g clotted cream
100g unsalted butter
sea salt & white pepper

for the sauce
25g unsalted butter
1 shallot, peeled and finely chopped
2 Cox's Orange Pippin apples, cored and cut into small wedges
80ml Calvados
30ml whipping cream
1 tsp balsamic vinegar
100ml chicken stock

PAN-FRIED CHICKEN FILLET AND WOODALL'S SPICY CUMBERLAND SALAMI CRISPS WITH PEA AND MINT PURÉE

for the purée
400g frozen garden peas
1 small bunch fresh mint,
*   stalks removed*
10ml chicken stock

for the chicken
12 chicken inner fillets
2 tbsps olive oil
sea salt & black pepper

for the salami crisps
80g Woodall's spicy
*   Cumberland salami*

to serve
150g wild rocket, washed and dried
100g Parmesan, shaved
2 tbsps olive oil

Serves 4: prep: 10 minutes/cook: 15-25 minutes

To make the purée, place the frozen peas, mint leaves and chicken stock in a saucepan and bring to the boil. Remove from the heat and using a stick blender, blend to a smooth purée.

To cook the chicken, drizzle the fillets with the olive oil, and season with a large pinch of salt and freshly cracked black pepper. Heat a frying pan on a medium to high heat and pan-fry the chicken, turning every 2 minutes, for 10-12 minutes. Ensure the centre reaches 75°C on your meat thermometer. Remove to a warm plate to rest for a few minutes.

To make the salami crisps, place a frying pan on a high heat and when almost smoking hot place the spicy Cumberland salami in the pan. Crisp up the salami on each side for 60-90 seconds. Remove the crisps to a plate topped with kitchen towel to soak up any excess oil.

To serve, place a large spoonful of pea purée in the centre of each of four bowls, top with three chicken fillets and four spicy Cumberland salami crisps. Garnish with a handful of wild rocket and sprinkle over the shaved Parmesan. Drizzle with olive oil.

CHARGRILLED CHICKEN WITH HALLOUMI, FLATBREAD AND HUMMUS

Serves 4: prep: 40 minutes/cook: 30 minutes

To make the flatbread, mix all the ingredients together in a bowl, bring together to form a dough then knead gently for 2 minutes. Split the mixture into 4 evenly-sized balls and, using plenty of flour, roll out to 2mm thick. Heat a griddle pan on a high heat until almost smoking and cook the flatbreads for 30-45 seconds on each side. The bread should be cooked but not overly crispy. When cooked, place on a wire rack to cool. The flatbreads can be stored in an airtight container if making in advance.

To make the hummus, place all the ingredients in a food processor, season with salt and freshly cracked black pepper and blitz to a smooth paste. Use a spatula to scrape down the sides and blend again to ensure no lumps. Set aside.

To cook the chicken, put the thighs in a mixing bowl and sprinkle on the ras el hanout and olive oil, season with salt and freshly cracked black pepper and mix ensuring the spices fully coat the thighs. Heat a griddle pan over a medium heat and when really hot add the thighs. Cook for 2 minutes before turning – this will give you great colour and flavour from the griddle pan. Continue turning every 2 minutes for a total of 8-10 minutes. Check with a meat thermometer that you have reached a core temperature of 75°C in the thickest part of the chicken. When cooked, transfer to a dish to rest whilst you char the halloumi. Using the same pan, char the halloumi for 90 seconds on each side.

To serve, warm the flatbreads in a hot oven for about 30 seconds, spread over a generous topping of smoked garlic hummus, add some lamb's lettuce and sprinkle over the pomegranate seeds. Slice the chicken thighs and place on top. Drizzle with olive oil.

for the flatbread
550g plain flour
1 tsp salt
½ tsp white caster sugar
½ tsp baking powder
50g natural yoghurt
1 tsp milk powder
30g vegetable oil
375ml skimmed milk
20g fresh coriander, finely chopped
80g rose harissa paste

for the hummus
400g chickpeas, drained
4 cloves smoked garlic, peeled
50g tahini
1 lime, juice and zest
60ml olive oil
sea salt & black pepper

for the chicken
8 boneless chicken thighs, skin-on
1 tbsp ras el hanout
sea salt & black pepper
4 tbsps olive oil
250g halloumi, sliced into 1cm
  thick slices

to serve
50g lamb's lettuce
1 pomegranate, seeds removed

DOUBLE DIP PORK
NOISETTE LOLLIPOPS

for the pork

*1 pork fillet, cut into 2cm
    thick noisettes
1 tbsp olive oil
sea salt & black pepper*

for the beetroot hummus

*400g chickpeas, drained
150g fresh cooked beetroot
2 cloves garlic, peeled
50g tahini
1 lime, juice and zest
60ml cold water
60ml olive oil
sea salt & black pepper*

for the pistachios

*125g peeled pistachios
sea salt*

Serves 4: prep: 15 minutes/cook: 10 minutes

To cook the pork, coat the pork noisettes in the olive oil, season with salt and freshly cracked black pepper. Heat a griddle pan until smoking over a high heat, add the noisettes to the pan and cook for 2 minutes on each side. Rest on a warm plate for two minutes. Place a skewer in each piece of pork ready for dipping.

To make the beetroot hummus, place the drained chickpeas, beetroot, garlic, tahini, lime juice and zest, water and olive oil in a food processor and blend to a smooth paste. Season to taste with salt and cracked black pepper.

To roast the pistachios, pre-heat the oven to 200°C/400°F/ gas mark 6. Place the pistachios in a tray and roast in the oven for 8-10 minutes, then sprinkle with the sea salt. Leave the nuts to cool, then roughly chop, leaving them quite chunky.

To serve, take the skewered pork noisette, dip into the beetroot hummus, then into the pistachio nuts, and eat!

FIRECRACKER CHICKEN

Serves 4: prep: 20 minutes/marinate: 2 hours/cook: 20-25 minutes

To marinade the chicken, place all the ingredients, apart from the chicken, in a bowl and mix well together. Add the chicken slices and mix well. Cover the dish with a lid or cling film and place in the fridge for a minimum of 2 hours or ideally overnight.

To cook the rice, wash the rice to remove any starch. Add 650ml water to the rice in a pan, season well with salt and bring to the boil. Stir well, place the lid tightly on top, turn off the heat and leave the rice to soak up the remaining liquid. When ready fluff up the rice with a fork for serving.

To cook the chicken, remove it from the marinade. Heat up a little vegetable oil in a large frying pan or wok over a medium to high heat until very hot. Add the chicken and brown on each side. Add the onion quarters and finely chopped chillies and soften for 90 seconds. Add the marinade and bring to a boil, then add the peppers and mangetout and cook for another 90 seconds. Finally, just before serving, add the chopped spring onions.

To serve, spoon some basmati rice into a bowl and top with the firecracker chicken. Sprinkle with toasted black sesame seeds.

for the chicken
4 x 150g Norfolk chicken breasts,
  sliced into 1cm thick slices
1 tbsp vegetable oil
1 red chilli, seeds removed
  and chopped finely
2 tbsps sriracha chilli sauce
4 garlic cloves, peeled and
  finely chopped
4 tbsps light soft brown sugar
3 tbsps light soy sauce
2 tbsps dark soy sauce
1 tbsp rice wine vinegar
1 tbsp tamarind paste
1 tbsp fish sauce
1 pinch of white pepper

for the stir-fry
2 tbsps vegetable oil, for cooking
1 large white onion, peeled
  and quartered
6 dried árbol chillies, finely chopped
1 habanero chilli, finely chopped
1 red pepper, seeds removed,
  sliced into thick batons
1 green bell pepper, seeds removed,
  sliced into thick batons
120g mangetout
1 bunch of spring onions,
  roughly chopped

for the rice
350g basmati rice
sea salt

to serve
2 tsps black sesame seeds, toasted

HAM HOCK AND
CAPER TERRINE

for the terrine

3 ham hocks, cured
10 peppercorns
3 bay leaves
½ onion
2 sticks celery
1 sprig thyme
2 sheets gelatine
40g small capers
1 small bunch of parsley, chopped

for the piccalilli

30g salt
1l water
1 red pepper, diced small
1 yellow pepper, diced small
½ cucumber, diced small
1 courgette, diced small
100g onion, finely chopped
¼ cauliflower, broken into
    small florets
2 stalks celery, thinly sliced
350ml white wine vinegar
½ chilli
75g caster sugar
2 tbsps horseradish
1 sprig thyme
1 bay leaf
20g cornflour
1 heaped tsp turmeric
35g Dijon mustard

to serve

sourdough toast
lamb's lettuce

Makes 1 terrine: prep: 25-30 minutes/cook: 6 hours

To make the terrine, in a large pan cover the ham hocks in water, add the peppercorns, bay leaves, onion, celery and thyme and bring to the boil; simmer for 4-5 hours until tender. Remove the hocks from the cooking liquor onto a tray, then place the pan back on to the heat and reduce the cooking liquor by half and put to one side. Soak the gelatine in cold water until soft, boil 500ml of the cooking liquor and add the gelatine. Put to one side and allow to cool. Shred the ham by hand into small pieces, removing any bone or chunks of fat. Place the capers and parsley in the bowl with the shredded ham, add some of the cooled cooking liquor until coated and mix well. Line a terrine mould or ramekins with cling film and press the ham in firmly. Cover and chill overnight until set.

To make the piccalilli, dissolve the salt in the water. Place the peppers, cucumber, courgette, onion, cauliflower and celery in a sealable container with the salted water and leave to soak overnight. Prepare a pickling liquor by mixing the vinegar, chilli, sugar, horseradish, thyme and bay leaf together in a saucepan and bring to the boil for 1 minute. Prepare a paste by mixing the cornflour, turmeric and mustard together in a bowl. Strain the pickling liquor and mix it into the paste mix, return to the boil whisking continuously for 1 minute to cook out the flour. Strain the soaked vegetables and discard any liquid, rinse well with fresh water. Remove the pickling liquor and paste from the heat and stir in the pickled vegetables. Chill the piccalilli and serve cold from the fridge. Any leftovers are best kept in an airtight jar in the fridge.

To serve, lightly toast some slices of sourdough bread. Remove the terrine from the fridge and slice into 1½ cm thick slices. Place a slice on a plate or board and serve with a large spoonful of piccalilli, lamb's lettuce and the toasted sourdough bread.

HOG ROAST BELLY BITES
WITH APPLE KETCHUP

Serves 4: prep: 10 minutes/sous vide: 12 hours/cook: 10-20 minutes

To make the belly bites, season the belly with the smoked sea salt and freshly cracked black pepper, then vacuum seal in a plastic pouch. Sous vide at 85°C for 12 hours, remove from the water bath, refresh in a sink of cold water to reduce the temperature quickly, then place in the fridge overnight pressed between two heavy items (such as heavy casserole dishes) to create a uniform shape for cutting.

To make the belly bites (without a sous vide machine), season the belly with the smoked sea salt and freshly cracked black pepper. Place in a roasting dish with a splash of pork stock, cover with tin foil and cook in the oven at 140°C/275°F/gas mark 1 for 5 hours. Remove from the oven and allow to cool to room temperature then chill down in the fridge, pressing between something heavy.

To make the crackle crumb, boil a kettle and place the scored rind on a cooling rack in or over the sink. Pour boiling water over the scored rind to open it up. Dry completely with paper towel and rub with sea salt. Place on a tray and bake in the oven for 40 minutes at 200°C/400°F/gas mark 6 until crisp. When cool, crush the rind into crumbs.

To make the apple ketchup, place the diced apples in a pan with the cider vinegar, sugar, cinnamon and vanilla pod cut in half and seeds scraped out and added. On a low heat so the apples do not colour cook down to a purée. Pass through a sieve or blend to ensure no lumps and a smooth texture.

To serve, cut the pork into small 2cm or 3cm squares, drizzle with oil, season with salt and pepper and pan fry in a frying pan, fat side down, for 2 minutes on a medium to high heat until the fat is golden brown. Transfer to a baking tray and roast in the oven at 200°C/400°F/gas mark 6 for 8-10 minutes to reheat without drying out the belly. Serve with the apple ketchup and crackle crumb.

for the belly bites
600g lean rindless pork belly
sea salt & black pepper

for the crackle crumb
150g pork rind
sea salt

for the apple ketchup
2 Bramley apples, peeled,
  core removed and diced
30ml cider vinegar
50g caster sugar
½ cinnamon stick
½ vanilla pod

MASTER STOCK BRAISED HAMPSHIRE PORK BELLY

for the master stock
3 litres water
8 garlic cloves, peeled and left whole
1 tsp Szechuan peppercorns
1 large lobe of ginger, sliced
8 shallots
3 tbsps coriander, with stalks
3 cinnamon sticks
8 star anise
1 tsp fennel seeds
3 cloves
150ml light soy sauce
100ml dark soy sauce
375ml Chinese Shaoxing wine
80g palm sugar
1.5kg rindless Hampshire pork
*   belly cut into 3 large squares*

for the sticky braising sauce
200ml strained master stock
50ml light soy sauce
100g light brown sugar
1 tsp five spice
3 tbsps rice wine vinegar
1 tbsps fish sauce

for the rice
200g basmati rice
sea salt

for the crispy shallots
200ml vegetable oil, for frying
3 banana shallots, peeled and sliced
*   into thin rings*
3 tbsps milk
100g plain flour, seasoned with salt
*   and cracked black pepper*

to serve
1 small bunch fresh coriander,
*   roughly chopped*
1 red chilli, thinly sliced
1 tbsp sesame seeds, toasted

Serves 4: prep: 20 minutes/cook: 2 hours 30 minutes

To make the master stock, place all the ingredients into a large stockpot, bring to the boil and simmer for 5 minutes. Submerge the pork belly in the master stock and gently simmer for 1½ hours, until tender but not falling apart. Remove the pork belly and set aside to cool. Once cool place the pork covered in the fridge overnight, Strain the master stock cool and reserve.

When the opportunity arises to re-use the master stock, replenish with 500ml cold water, fresh garlic, ginger, Szechuan peppercorns, cinnamon sticks, star anise, and shallots and coriander roots. Each time the stock is used, the depth of flavour is enhanced. To store, allow it to cool completely before straining through a fine sieve. It can be then be refrigerated or stored for longer in the freezer.

To braise the pork belly, slice the chilled pork belly into generous cubes - approximately 3cm to 4cm square. In a medium saucepan make the sticky braising sauce by heating 200ml of the master stock, the soy sauce, brown sugar and five spice over medium heat, stirring until sugar has dissolved. Add the rice wine vinegar and fish sauce, and then add the cubes of pork belly. Bring to a boil then reduce the heat. Simmer the pork for 25-30 minutes, until the sauce is thick and glossy and the pork is meltingly tender and rich.

To cook the rice, place the rice in a pan with 250ml of water and a large pinch of salt and stir well. Bring the rice to the boil, place the lid on the pan and turn off the heat. Let the rice stand for 20 minutes to soak up the liquid before fluffing up with a fork.

To make the crispy shallots, heat the oil in a large saucepan on a medium heat to around 170°C. Place the shallot rings in a bowl and add the milk. Mix the onions to ensure they have all been coated in milk. Drain off any excess milk and toss the shallots in the seasoned flour. Fry in the hot oil until brown and crispy. Remove from the oil and place on kitchen towel to soak up any excess oil.

To serve, arrange the pork with some cubes on their side displaying their succulent layers, others with the juicy fat facing up, on top of some basmati rice. Sprinkle with the shallots, coriander, chilli and sesame seeds.

PORK AND 'NDUJA MEATBALLS WITH SPICY TOMATO SAUCE

Serves 4: prep: 20 minutes/cook: 1 hour 30 minutes

To make the meatballs, thoroughly mix all the ingredients together, season with a large pinch of salt and freshly cracked black pepper. Separate the meat into approximately twelve 50g meatballs and using the palms of your hands roll the ball round to create a smooth finish. Place in the fridge covered with cling film to rest for 30 minutes before cooking.

To make the sauce, heat a little olive oil in a large saucepan over a medium heat and pan-fry the onion until softened, then add the garlic, chilli and 'nduja paste. Mix well and cook for 1 minute. Add the tinned tomatoes, mix through and then bring to a simmer. Turn the heat down so the sauce is just gently bubbling away and let the sauce reduce for an hour. Add the freshly chopped basil and season well with salt and freshly cracked black pepper.

To cook the meatballs, pan-fry the meatballs in a little sunflower oil on a medium to high heat to create a golden crust around the outside. When golden brown add the balls to the spicy tomato sauce and gently simmer for 20 minutes.

To serve, cook the fresh tagliatelle and toss in olive oil, finish with shaved parmesan and fresh basil leaves.

for the meatballs
500g pork mince (10% fat)
80g 'nduja paste
50ml water
5 stalks of fresh basil, roughly chopped, stalks included
4 garlic cloves, peeled and finely chopped
½ tsp ground fennel
sea salt & black pepper
2 tbsps vegetable oil, for cooking

for the sauce
2 tbsps olive oil
1 large onion, finely chopped
2 garlic cloves, peeled finely chopped
1 red chilli, finely chopped
90g 'nduja paste
3 x 400g tins of chopped tomatoes
3 stalks of fresh basil, roughly chopped, stalks included
sea salt & black pepper

to serve
360g fresh tagliatelle
2 tbsps olive oil
100g Parmesan, shaved
1 small bunch basil, stalks removed

SOY AND GINGER
CHICKEN LOLLIPOPS

for the chicken lollipops
500g chicken wings
50g grated fresh ginger
25g garlic, finely chopped
½ red chilli, finely chopped
2 tbsps vegetable oil, for cooking
50g dark soy sauce
50g light soy sauce
1 lime, juice and zest
50g honey

to garnish
1 large pinch of nigella seeds
6 spring onions, finely chopped

Serves 4: prep: 20 minutes/marinate: 2 hours/cook: 16-20 minutes

To make the chicken lollipops, carefully cut 360° around the top of the chicken wing releasing the meat and skin from the bone. Pull the meat down the bone of the wing turning the meat 'inside out' to create a lollipop shape, with the bone being the stick and a ball of meat at the other end. Place the lollipops in a bowl. In a hot wok lightly fry the ginger, garlic and chilli in a little vegetable oil. Pour into a bowl, add the soy sauces, lime juice, zest and honey, mix well. Pour this over the chicken wings and leave to marinate for 2 hours, covered, in the fridge.

To cook the lollipops, either pre-heat the oven to 200°C/400°F/gas mark 6 or prepare your barbecue ready for cooking. Take the wings out of the marinade and roast in the oven for 16 minutes until cooked and caramelised, or place on the barbecue turning every 90 seconds until cooked. Place on a plate and sprinkle with nigella seeds and sliced spring onions.

TERIYAKI PORK SKEWERS

Serves 4: prep: 20 minutes/marinate: 3 hours/cook: 15-25 minutes

To make the teriyaki sauce, combine all the ingredients in a saucepan and bring to a boil over medium heat. Reduce the heat to low and simmer for 10-15 minutes until the liquid reduces by half (it's okay if the sauce gets foamy towards the end; just remove from heat for a moment to check how much liquid has cooked off.) Once the teriyaki sauce is ready (when it coats the back of a spoon with a thin film), remove and strain the garlic, ginger and lemongrass. Allow the sauce to come to room temperature.

To make the marinade, add all the ingredients to a large bowl and stir. Add the pork pieces and turn to coat evenly with the marinade. Cover, and refrigerate for 3 hours.

To barbecue the pork, pre-heat a grill pan on a medium heat or prepare your barbecue. Thread three pieces of pork onto each skewer, alternating with 2 pieces of spring onion. Lightly oil the bars of the griddle pan or barbecue and cook for approximately 12-15 minutes, turning every two minutes and brushing regularly with the teriyaki sauce to get a rich, glossy glaze, until the meat is cooked through.

To serve, enjoy with some steamed basmati rice, or as part of a barbecue with a green salad and jacket potatoes.

for the teriyaki sauce

2 lemongrass stalks, finely chopped
250ml dark soy sauce
30ml light soy sauce
80ml mirin
40ml Chinese Shaoxing wine
80g demerara sugar
2 cloves of garlic, finely chopped
50g ginger, peeled and sliced
  into matchsticks

for the teriyaki marinade

30ml dark soy sauce
1 tbsp light soy sauce
1 tsp garlic purée
1 tsp ginger purée
2 tbsps sesame oil
1 tsp Korean red pepper flakes
1 pinch of white pepper
1 tbsp demerara sugar

for the pork

6 Hampshire pork loin steaks, thin
  cut, fat removed and cut into
  1.5cm by 3cm pieces
12 wooden skewers soaked in warm
  water for 30 minutes

to serve

6 spring onions cut
  into 3 cm lengths

STREET FOOD

120 — 171

WOOD-SMOKED MEATS
— Josh Ebsworth, Howard's Meat Co.

Cooking ribs and smoking meat is all about feel. It's about a love of the product, a knowledge and understanding of how smoke works and, above all, about the slow tick of time as the gentle, permeating heat of a wood fire does its business. Get it right and slow-cooked ribs are one of the finest things you'll ever eat.

Josh Ebsworth, of Howard's Meat Co, got a very good training in his craft whilst living in Texas and today, based in the London Fields area of North London at Netil Market, has become one of the leaders of a new British meat-smoking trend.

"I was lucky," Josh says about his experiences in America. "I was living in Austin, Texas, and I fell in love with the whole food culture. There's something about the place and the product and how life evolves around the smoker. There's nothing fussy about it. It's very home-style and that appeals to me. But it's also a craft that you have to learn. It's not easy and that's why there are very few really good places that do it properly.

"I got a job at an amazing rib restaurant called Micklethwait Craft Meats. I say restaurant but actually it's just a trailer with a smoker. However, don't be fooled by appearances: Tom Micklethwait is one of the best smokers in the USA.

"I spent eight months with Tom and loved every second. He set up the business with some friends who he'd met whilst working in a fine dining restaurant. I knew at once that I wanted to bring the craft home and when I got back in 2015 I got a friend to convert an old horse trailer and set up a stall. I called it the Horse Box Kitchen. Later it became Howard's Meat Co after my grandfather.

"It took me six months to even get close to what I experienced in Austin because I had to learn my smoker. It really is as simple as that. There are no temperature controls so you have to get to know the wood, the heat, the level of smoke and the time it takes to get the flavour you want.

"The wood is crucial. This is where the flavour comes from. You have to learn the way it burns, the heat it produces and the flavour it adds. It's a feel thing, and is one of the reasons why we are not very commercial. We couldn't cope with demand.

"We are also changing the process. I am always tinkering, trying to get a better product. And I experiment with different flavours and techniques. We cook all sorts of different meats. Pork ribs are popular, obviously. We also do enormous pork chops and smoked belly."

SMOKING IS A WORK OF
PASSION AND CREATIVITY
WITHIN A VERY NARROW
SKILL BASE. THERE ARE
VERY FEW OF US WHO
DO IT AS IT SHOULD BE
DONE BECAUSE IT'S HARD
WORK. BUT THE PAY-
OFF IS THE FACT THAT
WE GET LONG QUEUES
AND HAVE VERY DEVOTED
CUSTOMERS.

SMOKED PULLED
PORK CARNITAS

for the rub
200g coarsely cracked black pepper
60g salt
200g paprika
100g demerara sugar
20g chipotle powder
10g cumin
50g mustard powder
2 tbsps dried thyme

for the pork
3kg-5kg bone-in Boston butt
   pork shoulder
500ml fresh orange juice
5 cloves of garlic, peeled and sliced
3 jalapeno peppers, seeds removed
   and sliced
3 bay leaves
2 limes, quartered

to serve
8 flatbreads
1 medium red cabbage, finely sliced
150ml sriracha hot sauce
1 small bunch of parsley, stalks
   removed and roughly chopped

Serves 4: prep: 15 minutes/cook: 7-8 hours

Setting up your smoker may seem complicated but once you start practising and tweaking you will soon be the envy of all your friends at barbecues. First you are going to need a barbecue that you can smoke in. Webber make some great barbecues and they're not too expensive. As a basic rule, you need a kettle barbecue with a lid and vent holes both on the base and on the lid, and ideally it will have a built-in temperature gauge. The vent holes are important, both to allow control of the temperature inside, and to allow the smoke to escape so you don't end up with overly smoky, bitter-tasting meat. Charcoal is just as important as having the right barbecue. As with everything in life, you get what you pay for. If you buy cheap charcoal it probably won't last very long and will cause you more issues than buying the right stuff to start with. For low and slow cooking and smoking we suggest you buy good quality charcoal briquettes. Briquettes are compacted so you need less and they burn slower and longer than lumpwood charcoal, so are perfect for long smoking in your barbecue.

To set up your smoker, place 3-4 firelighters on one side in the bottom of the barbecue, and top with a generous amount of charcoal briquettes, ensuring everything is in one side of the base. Half open the vents on the top and bottom of the barbecue. Light the firelighters and allow the charcoal to burn for 10 minutes with the lid off, then place the lid on and allow the charcoal to burn and develop for at least 20 minutes. Place the cooking grill on and place a small oven dish filled with cold water on the side directly on top of the hot coals. This deflects the intense heat away from the meat and will create humidity within the barbecue to stop the meat from shrinking and drying out.

Place a handful of wood chips on top of the hot coals and replace the lid of the barbecue for 2 minutes to allow the temperature to increase. Close the vents so that they are one-third open, allowing enough oxygen in to keep the coals burning and enough smoke out so that you don't over-smoke the meat. You will have to adjust this to ensure you are hitting 140°C/275°F in your barbecue. You are now ready to cook. We suggest adding another handful of wood chips every 60-90 minutes to continue the smoking process during cooking.

To cook the pork, mix all the rub ingredients together and then rub into the pork until fully covered. Smoke the pork for 4 hours, keeping a constant temperature.

Pre-heat the oven to 150°C/300°F/gas mark 2. Transfer the pork shoulder to a deep-sided baking tray and add the orange juice, garlic, jalapenos, bay leaves and limes. Cover with tin foil and cook for 2½ hours. Remove the tin foil and, using two forks, shred the meat from the bone.

To serve, add a good amount of shredded pork to the flatbreads with red cabbage and sriracha hot sauce, and garnish with chopped parsley.

SMOKED CHAR SIU
BABY BACK RIBS

Serves 4: prep: 20 minutes/marinate: 4 hours/cook: 3-4 hours

To prepare the ribs, peel off the membrane from the rear of the baby back rib (this looks like a fatty layer of skin that can be easily peeled off in one piece); this allows the rub to penetrate the rib from both sides creating much more flavour. Season the ribs with the sea salt, cover and refrigerate for 4 hours.

To make the dry rub, combine all the ingredients together and rub both sides of the ribs.

To cook the ribs, set up your smoker (see page 127) to 140°C/275°F. Smoke the ribs for 2 hours, turning halfway through. After the 2 hours, wrap the ribs in tin foil, adding a piece of butter per rib, and cook for another 1½ hours.

To make the char siu dressing, combine all the ingredients in a bowl and mix well.

To finish the ribs, remove the tin foil and using a pastry brush apply char siu dressing liberally. Sear over hot coals for 45 seconds on each side, or until the dressing starts to bubble and crisp.

To serve, this can be eaten on its own or served as part of a barbecue, cut into individual ribs and drizzled with extra char siu dressing.

for the ribs
*4 racks Hampshire baby back
  pork ribs, about 500g each
4 tbsps fine sea salt
200g unsalted butter, cut into
  4 equal-sized pieces*

for the dry rub
*100g cracked black pepper
2 tsps Chinese five-spice
2 tsps garlic powder
2 tsps mustard powder
1 pinch of mace
1 pinch of allspice*

for the char siu dressing
*100g hoisin sauce
100g oyster sauce
100g mushroom soy sauce
100g honey
40g sriracha sauce*

ST LOUIS RIBS

for the ribs
1.5kg St Louis rib rack
1 tbsp olive oil
2 tbsps fine sea salt

for the dry rub
50g cracked black pepper
1 tbsp mustard powder
1 tsp coriander seed
1 tsp allspice
1 tsp freshly ground coffee beans
1 tsp garlic powder

for the jacket potatoes
4 large baking potatoes
unsalted butter

for the mother sauce
50g butter
2 jalapenos, roasted until soft
5 large tomatoes, diced
5 red bell peppers, seeds removed
  and diced
5 cloves of garlic, peeled and
  finely chopped
2 red onions, peeled and diced
1 dried ancho chilli, finely chopped
2 limes, zest and juice
1 tbsp smoked paprika
½ tbsp cumin
1 pinch of cayenne pepper

for the charred corn
2 corn on the cobs, skin removed
  and cut in half lengthways
2 tbsps corn oil
sea salt & black pepper
½ tsp cayenne pepper

Serves 4: prep: 30 minutes/marinate: 2 hours/cook: 4-5 hours

To make the dry rub, mix all the ingredients together and rub the mix into both sides of the ribs.

To marinade the ribs, coat the ribs with the olive oil, sprinkle over the sea salt and rub it all over the ribs. Cover and refrigerate for 2 hours.

To cook the ribs, set up your smoker (see page 127) to 140°C/275°F. Place the ribs bone side down and cook for 1½ hours. When done, turn the ribs over and cook for another 1½ hours until they have turned a mahogany colour. Wrap the rib rack in tin foil and return to the smoker for another 1½ hours. For those that don't mind a little cheating, or have other things to cook on the barbecue, this can be done in the oven at 170°C/325°F/gas mark 3 for 45 minutes. The ribs are done when you can push a toothpick through the meat will little resistance.

To bake the jacket potatoes, wrap the potatoes in tin foil and place in the barbecue smoker with the ribs and cook for the last 1½ hours of cooking. Just before serving slice a cross in the centre of the potatoes and add a little butter.

To make the mother sauce, heat a large frying pan on a medium heat, add the butter, roasted jalapenos, tomatoes, peppers, garlic, red onions and chilli, and lightly colour. Add the spices and lime and stir well. Gently simmer for 45 minutes, then using a stick blender blend into a coarse sauce.

To cook the corn, place the cobs in a mixing bowl, add the corn oil, cayenne pepper and a large pinch of salt and freshly cracked black pepper and toss the corn to fully coat. Heat a griddle pan until smoking hot over a medium to high heat then add the corn, turning when it starts to char. Cook for 7-10 minutes, until the corn is tender. Once charred on all sides remove from the pan and serve.

To serve, cut into individual ribs with a long sharp knife and serve with the mother sauce, charred corn and jacket potatoes.

BEER-BRINED
BARBECUED CHICKEN

Serves 4: prep: 20 minutes/marinate: 12 hours/cook: 1 hour 30 minutes

To brine the chicken, bring the beer, garlic, water and salt to a boil. Remove from the heat and allow to cool. Add the thyme and pour the brine into a sealable bag with the chicken. Push out as much air as possible while sealing and refrigerate overnight.

To barbecue the chicken, remove the chicken from the brine 2 hours before cooking and season with a large pinch of cracked black pepper.

Prepare the barbecue with plenty of coal so the chicken keeps a good temperature throughout cooking, and light: when the coals are ready they will be white in colour with no flames. Push the white-hot coals over to one side and place the chicken on the barbecue, breast side up, with the legs towards the coals.

Place the lid on and check the cooking temperature: it should be around 150°C/300°F. Cook until the internal temperature of the legs hits 75°C/150°F which will take approximately 2 hours. Every 20 minutes brush the chicken with olive oil to create a golden brown crispy skin.

To serve, season with a large pinch of sea salt and cracked black pepper, and garnish with the freshly chopped thyme and the lemon zest.
Serve with some roasted sweet potato wedges and a summer salad of green leaves, tomatoes and beetroot drizzled with a fresh vinaigrette.

for the chicken
1.7kg free range chicken
1 litre of Adnams Ghost Ship ale
1 garlic bulb, cut in half horizontally
200ml water
1 tbsp salt
*2 tbsps fresh thyme, stalks removed
    and finely chopped*
4 tbsps olive oil
sea salt & black pepper
*1 tbsp fresh thyme, stalks removed
    and finely chopped*
zest of 1 lemon

CHICKEN BURRITOS WITH LIME RICE, CHILLI CHEESE, TOMATO AND CHILLI SALSA AND SOUR CREAM

for the chicken
2 tsps smoked paprika
500g chicken breasts
sea salt & black pepper
1 white onion, peeled and
 finely chopped
2 garlic cloves, peeled and
 finely chopped
2 jalapeno chillies, seeds removed
 and finely chopped
1 tbsp vegetable oil
zest of 1 lime
½ tsp cumin
½ tsp oregano
100ml chicken stock

for the rice
200g basmati rice
sea salt & black pepper
2 limes, juice and zest

for the salsa
2 tomatoes, quartered, seeds
 removed and diced
1 red chilli, seeds removed
 and finely chopped
1 red onion, peeled and
 finely chopped
1 small bunch of fresh coriander,
 finely chopped
3 tbsps olive oil
sea salt & black pepper

to serve
4 soft tortillas
200g cheese with chilli, grated
200g sour cream

Serves 4: prep: 30 minutes/cook: 3 hours

To cook the chicken, set a slow cooker to high. Sprinkle the smoked paprika over the chicken breasts and season with a large pinch of salt and freshly cracked black pepper. In a saucepan lightly fry the onion, garlic and jalapeno chillies in a little vegetable oil. Once softened add to the slow cooker. In the same pan lightly fry the chicken breast to brown on both sides and, once browned, add to the slow cooker. Add the lime zest, cumin, oregano and chicken stock, add the lid and cook for 2 hours until tender.

To cook the rice, wash the rice to remove any excess starch. Put the rice into a saucepan and add 250ml water. Season with a large pinch of salt and freshly cracked black pepper and add the lime juice and zest. Bring to the boil stirring occasionally to ensure the rice does not catch on the bottom. Stir then put on the lid and turn off the heat. Leave for 15 minutes to allow the rice to soak up all of the liquid before fluffing up with a fork.

To make the salsa, mix the tomatoes, chilli, onion and fresh coriander with the olive oil and season with a large pinch of salt and freshly cracked black pepper.

To serve, pre-heat the oven to 180°C/350°F/gas mark 4. Wrap the tortillas in tin foil and place in the oven for 10 minutes.

Remove the chicken breasts from the slow cooker and pull the meat with two forks to create long strands. Return the meat to the liquid in the slow cooker and mix together.

Build your burritos with the lime rice, pulled chicken, cheese, sour cream and salsa. Fold in the ends of the burrito, roll up in tin foil, place in the oven for 5 minutes, then serve.

CHIMICHURRI CHICKEN
THIGH BURGER

Serves 4: prep: 20 minutes/marinate: 1 hour/cook: 15-25 minutes

To marinate the chicken, place the chicken thighs in a bowl and add the garlic, chilli and olive oil, season with a large pinch of salt and freshly cracked black pepper. Mix thoroughly to coat all the chicken and leave to marinate for 1 hour covered in the fridge.

To cook the chicken, heat a griddle pan over a medium to high heat. When close to smoking hot, add the chicken thighs and cook for 12 minutes turning every 2 minutes. Using a meat thermometer, check the temperature of the thickest point of the chicken - it should reach 75°C.

To make the chimichurri, place all the ingredients into a food processor and blend to a smooth sauce.

To serve, coat both insides of the toasted seeded burger bun with mayonnaise. Place two thighs on top of the bottom half of the bun with a large spoonful of chimichurri dressing and a handful of wild rocket. Top with the burger bun lid and get stuck in!

for the chicken
8 chicken thighs, boneless and skinless
2 garlic cloves, peeled and finely chopped
1 red chilli, seeds removed and finely chopped
4 tbsps olive oil
sea salt & black pepper

for the chimichurri
40g fresh flat leaf parsley
1 tsp dried oregano
4 garlic cloves, peeled
1 red chilli, stalk and seeds removed
2 tbsps red wine vinegar
8 tbsps olive oil

to serve
4 seeded burger buns, cut in half and toasted
100g mayonnaise
150g wild rocket, washed and dried

DANDAN NOODLES

for the pork

2 tbsp vegetable oil
500g pork mince
5 garlic cloves, finely chopped
2 red chillies, finely chopped
180g sweet chilli sauce
120g light soy sauce
100g hoisin sauce

for the noodles

600g egg noodles, pre-soaked in
*   cold water*
30g fresh coriander, roughly chopped
1 bunch spring onions, thinly sliced

to serve

80g cashew nuts, roughly chopped
1 tbsp black onion seeds

Serves 4: prep: 10 minutes/cook: 15 minutes

To cook the pork, in a wok or frying pan on a medium heat add the vegetable oil and fry the mince, stirring to break it down. Fry until turning dry and brown. Add the garlic and chilli and fry for 2 minutes stirring occasionally. Add the sweet chilli, soy and hoisin sauces and fry for another minute.

To cook the noodles, drain the noodles from the cold water and add with the coriander and three-quarters of the spring onions to the pork mixture in the wok or frying pan. Fry for a further 2 minutes, gently turning over the noodles to coat with the mince and sauce mixture.

To serve, place the noodles in a bowl sprinkled with the remaining chopped spring onions, cashew nuts and black onion seeds.

GARLIC, THYME AND ROSEMARY PORK TOMAHAWK

Serves 4: prep: 5 minutes/cook: 12-15 minutes

To cook the tomahawks, pre-heat the oven to 180°C/350°F/gas mark 4. Place the tomahawks on a tray and coat on both sides with the oil, season with plenty of salt and freshly cracked black pepper.

Heat up a griddle pan over a high heat until smoking. Place the chops on the griddle for 90 seconds on each side until caramelised. Turn the heat off, add the sliced garlic, thyme, rosemary and butter and allow the butter to melt and the garlic and herbs to start cooking. After 2 minutes remove the chops to a baking tray and pour over the butter, garlic and herbs.

Place in the pre-heated oven for 6-8 minutes. Do not over-cook the pork; check with a meat thermometer that the thickest part of the meat has reached 70°C. Let the chops rest for 2 minutes on a warm plate before serving.

To make the apple ketchup, place the apple into a saucepan with the cider vinegar, sugar, vanilla pod and seeds and the butter. Cook over a low heat, stirring occasionally to break down the apple to a purée; this should take around 10-12 minutes. Pass through a sieve or blend with a stick blender to achieve a smooth apple ketchup.

To make ultimate mash, place the potatoes in a pan of water with a pinch of salt. Bring to the boil, simmer for 15-20 minutes until tender. Whilst the potatoes are cooking heat up the cream and butter with a pinch of salt and pepper. When the butter has melted, stir in and remove from the heat. When the potato is cooked pass through a ricer into a bowl. Mix the butter and cream mixture through and again season to taste with salt and pepper.

To serve, place the tomahawks on a warmed plate and enjoy with ultimate mash and apple ketchup.

for the tomahawks
4 pork tomahawk chops
60g vegetable oil
sea salt & black pepper
2 cloves garlic, thinly sliced
4 sprigs thyme
2 sprigs rosemary
100g unsalted butter, roughly diced

for the apple ketchup
190g Bramley apple, peeled and diced
20ml cider vinegar
25g sugar
1 vanilla pod, cut in half
  and seeds removed
20g unsalted butter

for ultimate mash
1kg Maris Piper potatoes, peeled and
  chopped into evenly-sized pieces
90g clotted cream
100g unsalted butter
sea salt & white pepper

GOCHUJANG PORK BURGER WITH CUCUMBER KIMCHI

for the burger
1 large pinch of salt
2 tbsps water
500g pork mince
2 tbsps breadcrumbs
2 garlic cloves, finely chopped
1 large red chilli, finely chopped
1 small bunch of fresh coriander,
    roughly chopped
1 pinch of white pepper
60g gochujang paste
60g Korean red pepper flakes
2 tbsps vegetable oil, for cooking

for the kimchi
1 cucumber
1 carrot
4 spring onions, finely chopped
1 clove of garlic, finely chopped
1 pak choi, roughly chopped
1 tsp Korean red pepper flakes
1 tbsp gochujang paste
2 tbsps rice wine vinegar
1 small bunch coriander, roughly
    chopped, stalks included
sea salt & black pepper

for the Korean mayo
120g mayonnaise
60g gochujang paste
1 tsp red pepper flakes
1 tbsp fresh coriander, finely chopped

to serve
4 brioche burger buns, halved
    and toasted under the grill

Serves 4: prep: 30 minutes/cook: 12-15 minutes

To make the burgers, dissolve the salt in the water, add to the pork mince and work with your hands in a bowl for 2 minutes. Add the rest of the ingredients apart from the Korean red pepper flakes and mix for one minute. Create 4 evenly-sized balls of burger meat and using a ring mould or pastry cutter lightly greased with oil mould the meat balls to make burgers. Once shaped, roll the edges of the burger in the Korean red pepper flakes and cover with cling film on a tray. Put in the fridge to firm up for a minimum of 1 hour before cooking.

To make the kimchi, using a peeler, peel long strips of cucumber until you reach the inside seeded layer of the cucumber, then turn and peel again. Discard the seeded part (or chop up and use in salad). Peel strips of carrot in the same way. Mix all the cucumber kimchi ingredients together, season with a large pinch of salt and freshly cracked black pepper, cover and refrigerate until needed.

To cook the burgers, pre-heat the oven to 180°C/350°F/gas mark 4. Lightly oil the burgers with the vegetable oil, heat up a griddle pan on a medium to high heat and griddle on both sides for 2 minutes to achieve nice-looking griddle lines and some caramelisation. Place the burgers on a non-stick oven tray and put in the oven for 8 minutes.

To make the Korean mayo, mix the mayo with the gochujang, red pepper flakes and chopped coriander.

To serve, spread a spoonful of Korean mayo on both cut sides of the toasted brioche bun, top the burger with cucumber kimchi and get yourself a napkin! These are great with some sweet potato fries.

INDIAN-SPICED PULLED PORK WITH ONION BHAJIS AND MANGO CHUTNEY

Serves 6: prep: 30 minutes/cook: 5 hours

To cook the pork, pre-heat oven to 140°C/275°F/ gas mark 1. Rinse the pork shoulder under cold water, dry with paper towel and place in a roasting tray. Rub 1 teaspoon of salt and the turmeric over the joint and allow to stand while you make the sauce.

Place a pan on a medium heat and add the ghee or butter. Once melted add the onion and fry until nicely browned. Add the garlic, ginger and spices to the pan heat on a low to medium heat for 1 minute. Add the tinned tomatoes, honey and water, simmer for 5 minutes on a low heat, season with a large pinch of salt and freshly cracked black pepper and pour over the pork. Cover and place in the oven for 5 hours.

To make the bhajis, sift the flour into a bowl, then stir in the butter or ghee and lemon juice to make a double cream consistency. Stir in the spices, herbs and salt and finally the onions until well coated.

Heat the oil or set the temperature on a deep-fat fryer to 180°C. Divide the mixture into 36 small balls and deep-fry until golden brown. Remove from the oil onto kitchen towel to soak up any excess oil. Season with salt.

To make the chutney, heat the oil on a low heat in a deep saucepan, add the onion and slowly fry until softened without colour. Stir in the ginger and continue cooking for a further 4 minutes, then stir in all the spices and fry for a further 4 minutes. Add the apple and 250ml water, cover the pan and simmer for 15 minutes. Stir in the mango and chilli and continue cooking for another 20 minutes until the apple has broken down and the mango is tender. Pour in the vinegar, stir in the sugar and salt, and reduce, uncovered, over a medium to high heat for 30 minutes. Make sure you stir regularly to avoid it burning. Once it looks pulpy, remove from the heat. Place in a Kilner jar or other airtight container and keep in the refrigerator. Bring to room temperature before serving.

To serve, when the pork is cooked, allow it to rest for 10 minutes then gently pull it apart with two forks. Mix through some juices from the baking tray to enhance the flavour. Place some pulled pork on top of the bhajis followed by a spoonful of mango chutney and drizzle with natural yoghurt, finally sprinkle with the finely chopped coriander.

for the pulled pork
1kg Hampshire pork neck
   fillet, rindless
1 tsp turmeric
2 tbsps ghee or butter
1 red onion
7 large garlic cloves, finely chopped
1 small lobe of ginger, finely diced
7 cardamom pods, crushed
1 tsp coriander seeds, crushed
3 curry leaves
2 tsps curry powder
1 can chopped tomatoes
1 tbsp honey
250ml water
sea salt & black pepper
120ml natural yoghurt
1 small bunch of coriander

for the onion bhajis
180g gram flour
2 tbsp ghee or melted butter
½ lemon juice
1 tsp turmeric
2 tsp cumin seeds
½ tsp fennel seeds
3 hot green chillis, finely chopped
3 tsps ginger
4 cloves garlic, finely chopped
30g coriander, roughly chopped
4 medium white onions, thinly sliced
2 large red onion, thinly sliced
1 litre vegetable oil, for frying
1 large pinch of salt

for the chutney
1 tbsp sunflower oil
1 white onion, thinly sliced
20g ginger, peeled and grated
5 cardamom pods
1 cinnamon stick
½ tsp cumin seed
½ tsp coriander seeds
½ tsp turmeric
1 Bramley apple, peeled, cored, diced
500gm mango, peeled and diced
½ red chilli, finely chopped
175ml white wine vinegar
150g golden caster sugar
1 tsp salt

INDONESIAN PORK FILLET SATAY WITH QUINOA SALAD

for the satay sauce
1 tbsp vegetable oil
2 garlic cloves, peeled and
*   finely chopped*
1 red chilli, seeds removed and
*   finely chopped*
1 small lobe of ginger, peeled and
*   finely chopped*
75ml dark soy sauce
400g coconut milk
1 lime, juice and zest
120g crunchy peanut butter

for the soy-glazed peanuts
40g unsalted peanuts
25g light soy sauce

for the pork
8 Breckland pork fillet medallions,
*   about 75g each*
2 tbsps olive oil
sea salt & black pepper

for the salad
3 medium-sized carrots, peeled,
*   then cut into ribbons*
1 small red chilli, seeds removed
*   and finely diced*
3 spring onions, finely sliced
4 radishes, finely sliced
240g ready cooked quinoa
30ml light soy sauce

to serve
4 spring onions, finely sliced

Serves 4: prep: 20 minutes/cook: 15-20 minutes

To make the satay sauce, heat a frying pan over a medium heat, add a little vegetable oil and add the garlic, chilli and ginger and lightly fry. Add the soy sauce, coconut milk, lime juice and zest and the peanut butter. Bring to a simmer while stirring, then keep warm until ready to use.

To make the soy-glazed peanuts, pre-heat the oven to 180°C/350°F/ gas mark 4. Put the peanuts into a small baking tray and mix with the soy sauce, place in the pre-heated oven for 5 minutes stirring halfway through. Remove from the oven and allow to cool.

To cook the pork, heat a frying pan on a medium to high heat. Coat the medallions with oil, season with salt and freshly cracked black pepper, then pan-fry for 3 minutes on each side. Allow the meat to rest on a warm plate for two minutes before serving.

To make the salad, mix the carrot ribbons, chilli, spring onion and radishes together. Empty the quinoa into a pan and heat with the soy sauce and 3 tablespoons of water. Mix through the carrot, spring onion and chilli mixture.

To serve, place a big spoonful of the quinoa salad on the middle of a plate, top with two sliced medallion steaks, spoon over a generous amount of satay sauce then scatter with the soy glazed peanuts and garnish with spring onions.

JERK CHICKEN, RICE AND PEAS WITH BLACK BEAN PURÉE

Serves 4: prep: 20 minutes/marinate: 1-12 hours/cook: 45 minutes

To marinate the chicken, mix all the marinade ingredients together in a bowl to a smooth paste, place the scored chicken legs on a tray and rub the marinade over the chicken ensuring an even cover all over. Ideally leave overnight for the best flavour; marinate for 60 minutes as a minimum.

To cook the chicken, pre-heat the oven to 170°C/325°F/gas mark 3. Heat the vegetable oil in a frying pan over a medium heat and pan-fry the jerk legs for 8-10 minutes, turning occasionally, until golden and crispy. Be careful not to burn the marinade on the outside of the chicken. Transfer to an oven tray, cover with tin foil and cook in the oven for 35 minutes or until cooked thoroughly through; check with a meat thermometer – the centre of the chicken needs to be 75°c.

To make the black bean purée, fry the chopped onion and garlic in a little vegetable oil until soft. Transfer to a blender, add the rest of the purée ingredients, season with salt and freshly cracked black pepper and blend to a smooth paste. Serve hot or cold.

To make the rice, while the chicken is in the oven, rinse the rice in some cold water. Add all the ingredients except the black and kidney beans, season with a large pinch of salt and freshly cracked black pepper and bring to the boil. Drain the beans and add to the rice mixture, stir in and bring back to the boil. Put a lid on the pan and then turn off the heat. After 10 minutes stir the rice with a fork, then put the lid back on and let stand for another 5 minutes.

To serve, drizzle some of the juices from the chicken over the meat and serve with a pot of black bean purée and rice.

for the marinade
2 Scotch bonnet chillies, deseeded and finely chopped
2 limes, juice and zest
40g fresh thyme, stalks removed and chopped
3 garlic cloves, peeled and finely chopped
1 tsp ground cloves
1 tsp ground cinnamon
1 tsp ground nutmeg
2 tsps ground allspice
½ tsp ground black pepper
½ tsp salt

for the chicken
2 tbsps vegetable oil
4 large chicken legs, skin on and deeply scored with a knife

for the black bean purée
1 medium onion, finely diced
2 garlic cloves, finely diced
1 tbsp vegetable oil
400g black beans, drained and rinsed
1 tsp chilli powder
½ tsp ground cumin
½ tsp ground black pepper
1 tbsp fresh coriander, roughly chopped
200ml coconut milk
2 tbsps olive oil
sea salt & black pepper

for the rice
200g basmati rice
400ml coconut milk
1 tbsp fresh thyme, stalks removed
1 tsp allspice
2 cloves garlic, finely chopped
2 spring onions, thinly sliced
sea salt & black pepper
400g black beans, drained and rinsed
200g kidney beans, drained and rinsed

for the chicken

100ml buttermilk
1 heaped tbsp gochujang paste
1 tsp Korean red pepper flakes
8 Norfolk chicken thighs,
*   deboned, skin on*
1 litre vegetable oil, for frying
75g cornflour
150g flour
1 tsp salt
1tsp baking powder

for the sauce

1 tbsp olive oil
50g ginger, peeled and grated
4 garlic cloves, peeled and grated
2 limes, juice and zest
40ml light soy sauce
40ml rice wine vinegar
80g honey
100g gochujang paste
½ tsp sea salt
1 tsp Korean red pepper flakes
sea salt & black pepper

to serve

2 spring onions
1 tbsp black onion seeds
30g cashews, roasted and chopped

Serves 4: prep: 20 minutes/marinate: 12 hours/cook: 8-10 minutes

To marinate the chicken, mix together the buttermilk, gochujang paste and red pepper flakes and coat the chicken with the marinade. Cover tightly with cling film and refrigerate for 12 hours. Remove the chicken from the marinade and drain off any excess liquid.

To make the sauce, heat the olive oil on medium to low heat and gently fry the ginger and garlic until they are starting to colour. Add the remaining sauce ingredients, season with salt and freshly cracked black pepper and bring to a gentle simmer on a medium heat. Once simmering, remove from the heat.

To fry the chicken, heat the oil in a deep-fat fryer to 170°C/375°F. Mix together the cornflour, flour, salt, red pepper and baking powder, and coat the chicken thoroughly all over.

Cook the chicken in the fryer for roughly 8 minutes, until the coating is a lightly golden colour and crisp. Be careful that the heat isn't too high as you don't want the coating going too dark before the chicken has cooked through. Check with a meat thermometer that the chicken has reached 75°C in the thickest part.

To serve, slice each piece of chicken in half and drizzle the sauce over the top. Garnish with finely sliced spring onions, black onion seeds and chopped cashews.

KOREAN PORK BELLY BAO BUNS WITH CUCUMBER KIMCHI AND CRISPY SHALLOTS

Serves 4: prep: 30 minutes/marinate: 24 hours/cook: 1 hour 45 minutes

To marinate the pork, mix all the marinade ingredients together and pour into a container that will comfortably hold the belly pork. Pat the pork skin totally dry with kitchen paper. Place the pork on top of the marinade, taking care not to get any of it on the top skin of the belly as this will burn when cooking in the oven. Cover with cling film and refrigerate for 24 hours.

To cook the pork, pre-heat your oven to 150°C/300°F/gas mark 2. Remove the belly from the marinade and sit on top of a wire rack on a deep baking tray. Add 200ml water to the marinade mix, stir together, then pour into the tray under the pork – it shouldn't touch the bottom of the belly and, again, be careful not to get any on the rind of the pork as it will burn. Spread the table salt evenly on top of the belly skin. Place the tray carefully in the oven on the top shelf for 70 minutes. Remove from the oven, and increase the temperature to 230°C/450°F/gas mark 8. Lift off the crust of salt from the top of the belly and discard.

Line another tray with non-stick greaseproof paper and place the belly on the tray, discarding the liquid from the previous tray. Lightly brush the rind with olive oil and sprinkle with a little salt. When the oven reaches temperature put the belly back in for 30-35 minutes until golden brown with bubbly crackling. Allow to rest for 10 minutes before slicing.

To make the kimchi, using a peeler, peel long strips of cucumber until you reach the inside seeded layer of the cucumber, then turn and peel again. Discard the seeded part (or chop up and use in salad). Peel strips of carrot in the same way. Mix all the cucumber kimchi ingredients together, season with a large pinch of salt and freshly cracked black pepper, cover and refrigerate until needed.

To make the crispy shallots, soak the shallot rings in the milk for 5 minutes. Drain off the milk then toss in seasoned flour to create a coating. Heat the vegetable oil in a pan and shallow fry until golden and crispy. Remove onto paper towel to take away any excess oil and sprinkle with a little salt.

To serve, steam the bao buns as instructed on the packet, slice the belly, and serve with a large spoonful of cucumber kimchi and a sprinkling of crispy shallots and Korean red pepper flakes.

for the marinade
120g gochujang paste
2 garlic cloves, peeled and finely chopped
60g ginger, finely chopped
80ml light soy sauce
60ml rice wine vinegar
2 limes, juice and zest
1 tbsp Korean red pepper flakes
50g honey

for the pork belly
1.5kg Breckland pork belly, rind on, unscored (needs to be even in thickness)
200g table salt
1 tbsp olive oil

for the cucumber kimchi
1 cucumber
1 carrot
4 spring onions, finely chopped
1 clove of garlic, finely chopped
1 pak choi, roughly chopped
1 tsp Korean red pepper flakes
1 tbsp gochujang paste
2 tbsps rice wine vinegar
1 small bunch coriander, roughly chopped, stalks included
sea salt & black pepper

for the crispy shallots
3 banana shallots, peeled and sliced into thin rings
3 tbsps milk
100g plain flour, seasoned with salt and cracked black pepper
200ml vegetable oil
sea salt

to serve
16 steamed bao buns
1 tsp Korean red pepper flakes

PAPRIKA PORK FILLET POT

for the pork

2 tbsps vegetable oil
600g Hampshire pork fillet, diced
220g white onion, peeled and
    thinly sliced
150g red pepper, seeds removed
    and sliced
150g green pepper, seeds removed
    and sliced
2 garlic cloves, peeled and
    finely chopped
70ml brandy
1 tbsp paprika
1 tbsp smoked paprika
300ml chicken stock
1 tbsp tomato purée
100g crème fraîche
½ lemon, juiced

for the rice

200g basmati rice
sea salt

to serve

80g crème fraiche
1 small bunch of chives, cut into
    2cm lengths

Serves 4: prep: 10 minutes/cook: 25-30 minutes

To cook the pork, heat half the oil in a large frying pan on a medium to high heat, add the diced pork tenderloin and cook till the meat is slightly coloured, but not fully cooked. Remove the pork and any juices from the pan and set aside in a bowl. Pour the other half of oil into the pan and add the onions, red peppers, green peppers and garlic and fry, stirring occasionally until softened and lightly coloured. Add the brandy to the hot pan and cook for 1 minute. Combine the two paprikas and stir into the onion, pepper and garlic mix. Pour in the chicken stock and tomato purée. Stir the mix until it starts to thicken and comes to the boil. Reduce the heat and stir in the crème fraîche and lemon juice and simmer for a further 2 minutes. Return the pork to the pan and cook for 5 minutes until it's fully cooked but remains soft and tender.

To cook the rice, place the rice in a pan with 250ml water and a pinch of salt and stir well together. Bring the rice to the boil, place the lid on the pan and turn off the heat. Leave for 20 minutes to soak up the liquid before fluffing up the rice with a fork.

To serve, drizzle the paprika pork with crème fraiche, sprinkle with the chives and serve with the rice.

PIRI PIRI CHICKEN WITH SWEET POTATO FRIES AND YORKSHIRE CHIP SPICE

Serves 4: prep: 20 minutes/marinate: 1 hour/cook: 1 hour

To marinate the chicken, place all the ingredients in a food processor and blend to a smooth paste. Place the chicken pieces in a mixing bowl and pour over the piri piri marinade, mixing to ensure it totally covers the chicken pieces, then cover with cling film and leave in the fridge for a minimum of 1 hour.

To cook the chicken, pre-heat the oven to 180°C/350°F/gas mark 4. Place the chicken pieces skin side up on a non-stick baking tray and pour over any excess marinade from the bowl. Roast in the oven for 45-60 minutes until the core temperature of the biggest piece, checked with a meat thermometer, reaches 75°C. Once cooked, remove from the oven and serve immediately.

To cook the corn, place the cobs in a mixing bowl and add the corn oil, salt, pepper and cayenne pepper and toss the corn to fully coat. Heat a griddle pan on a medium to high heat until smoking hot then add the corn, turning when it starts to char. Once charred on all sides remove from the pan and serve.

To make the chip spice, mix all the ingredients together in a bowl.

To cook the fries, heat the oil in a deep fat fryer to 190°C/375°F. Coat the sweet potato fries with the potato starch in a mixing bowl. When the fryer is up to temperature cook the fries until golden brown; this should take around 5-6 minutes. Place in a bowl lined with kitchen towel and sprinkle with the chip spice.

To serve, place the chicken, corn and fries onto a large wooden board and serve as a sharing platter in the middle of the table.

for the marinade
2 red bird's-eye chillies, stalk and seeds removed
2 Scotch bonnet red chillies, stalk and seeds removed
5 cloves garlic, peeled
1 lemon, juice and zest
1 lime, juice and zest
3 tbsps white wine vinegar
1 large bunch parsley, stalks included
1 tbsp smoked paprika
1 tsp dried oregano
2 tsps demerara sugar

for the chicken
2kg chicken butchered down to breasts, drumsticks, thighs and wings

for the charred corn
2 corns on the cob, skin removed and cut in half lengthways
2 tbsps corn oil

for the chip spice
1 tbsp smoked sea salt
1 tbsp ground paprika
1 tsp brown sugar
½ tsp black pepper
1 tsp ground garlic
1 tsp ground cumin
½ tsp cayenne pepper

for the fries
1 litre vegetable oil, for frying
1kg sweet potatoes, skin on, sliced into thin fries
80g potato starch

PORK FUSION TACO

for the pork

4 pork loin medallions,
*   cut into thin strips*
1 tsp wasabi paste
40g ginger, peeled and grated
zest of 2 limes
1 tbsp light soy sauce
1 tbsp olive oil

for the slaw

20g miso paste
90g crème fraiche
150g mangetout, finely sliced
150g edamame soya beans, cooked
1 large carrot, grated
juice of 1 lime
sea salt & black pepper

for the sauce

100g sriracha sauce
3 limes, juice and zest
1 tbsp dark soy sauce
20g yuzu juice

to serve

8 soft taco shells
100g radish, grated

Serves 4: prep: 15 minutes/marinate: 2 hours/cook: 10 minutes

To marinate the pork, mix the pork strips, wasabi paste, grated ginger, lime zest, soy sauce and olive oil together then cover with cling film and refrigerate for 2 hours.

To cook the pork, when marinated, heat a frying pan over a high heat until smoking, then add the pork. Cook until caramelised, tossing the pork in the pan – the strips should take 4-5 minutes to cook through. Remove from the heat.

For the slaw, in a bowl mix the miso paste and crème fraiche together until well mixed. Add the sliced mangetout, edamame beans, carrot, lime juice, season with a pinch of salt and freshly cracked black pepper and mix together.

For the sauce, mix all the ingredients together in a bowl.

To serve, pre-heat the oven to 180°C/350°F/gas mark 4. Wrap the soft tacos in tin foil and place in the oven for 5 minutes while cooking the pork. Place all the ingredients in the middle of the table in bowls – take a taco and place in some slaw, pork strips, radish and drizzle with sauce, roll up the taco and eat!

PORK RAGU BIANCO

Serves 4: prep: 25 minutes/cook: 15–20 minutes

To make the meatballs, combine the marjoram and nutmeg in a mixing bowl, season with a pinch of salt and freshly cracked black pepper, add the mince and mix well. Shape the mixture into small 3cm bite-sized balls and dust in the flour. Heat a frying pan on a medium to high heat with the olive oil and fry the meatballs on a high heat for 4 minutes, turning every minute until golden on the outside, then remove from the heat and place the meatballs in a tray lined with kitchen towel.

To fry the breadcrumbs, place the butter into a frying pan and melt on a medium heat. When foaming add the panko and fry gently, stirring continuously until lightly golden. Transfer to a bowl then mix in the rest of the ingredients, season with a pinch of salt and freshly cracked black pepper and set aside.

To make the sauce, heat the olive oil in a frying pan on a medium heat. Sweat the shallot, celery and carrot. Add the bay leaves, thyme, orange and lemon zest and cook for another 5 minutes. Add in the garlic and cook for a further 2 minutes. Then add the wine and stock and reduce by three-quarters until thickened. Grate in the Parmesan, then add the meatballs back to the pan and coat well with the sauce.

For the pasta, cook the pasta in boiling salted water for 10 minutes until just cooked.

To serve, drain the pasta, and add it to the meatballs and sauce. Serve piping hot, garnished with the breadcrumbs and the freshly chopped parsley.

for the meatballs
1 tsp ground marjoram
1 tsp ground nutmeg
sea salt & black pepper
500g pork mince (5% fat)
75g plain flour, for dusting
2 tbsp olive oil

for the breadcrumbs
20g unsalted butter
40g panko breadcrumbs
½ lemon zest
½ orange zest
10g fresh parsley, chopped
20g Parmesan, grated
sea salt & black pepper

for the sauce
2 tbsp olive oil
2 shallots, peeled, finely diced
2 celery sticks, finely diced
1 carrot, peeled, finely diced
2 bay leaves
4 thyme sprigs
zest of ½ orange
zest of ½ lemon
4 garlic cloves, peeled, finely chopped
150ml white wine
100ml chicken stock
50g Parmesan

for the pasta
500g conchiglie pasta
1 tsp salt
1 small bunch parsley, chopped

PULLED PORK ROLL
WITH ROSE HARISSA AND
POMEGRANATE MOLASSES

for the pork

*2.2kg Hampshire pork shoulder,
  boneless and rindless*
25g salt
25g demerara sugar
20g pomegranate molasses
1 tbsp smoked paprika

for the rose harissa

100g dried ancho chilli
20g dried árbol chilli
1 tsp cumin seeds
1 tsp coriander seeds
1 tsp caraway seeds
4 cloves garlic, peeled
40g sundried tomatoes
40g preserved lemon
1 tsp dried mint
3 tbsps olive oil
1 tbsp dried rose petals

for the hummus

400g chickpeas, drained
4 cloves smoked garlic, peeled
50g tahini
1 lime, juice and zest
60ml olive oil
sea salt & black pepper

to serve

6 large seeded crusty bread rolls
150g wild rocket

Serves 4: prep: 25 minutes/marinate: 26 hours/cook: 5 hours

To brine the pork, mix the salt, sugar, molasses and paprika together with 180g of water using a whisk until the sugar and salt have dissolved. Place the joint of pork in a vacuum bag with the brine, vacuum seal and leave for 24 hours in the fridge.

To make the rose harissa, place the dried chillies in a bowl, cover with boiling water and leave to soak for 10 minutes. Toast the spices in a frying pan over a medium heat, tossing occasionally to prevent burning, for about 2 minutes until the spices are releasing aromas. Grind the spices into a powder in a pestle and mortar. Drain the chillies (keep the water). Combine all the ingredients except the chilli water and rose petals in a food processor and blend to a smooth paste. Add some of the chilli water to create a paste the consistency of thick double cream. Add the petals and mix.

To roast the pork, remove from the brine and coat in the rose harissa paste; leave for another 2 hours, covered, in the fridge.

Pre-heat the oven to 140°C/275°F/gas mark 1. Place the joint onto a wire rack in a baking tray and cover with tin foil. Cook for 5 hours until tender and falling apart. Pull the meat apart into long meaty strands with two forks; pour over any liquid from the bottom of the tray and mix in with the meat.

To make the hummus, place all the ingredients in a food processor, season with a large pinch of salt and freshly cracked black pepper and blitz to a smooth paste. Use a spatula to scrape down the sides and blend again to ensure there are no lumps. Set aside.

To serve, spread plenty of smoked garlic hummus over both cut sides of a bread roll. Generously fill with pulled pork and fresh wild rocket.

SICHUAN CHICKEN
AND PEPPER STIR-FRY

Serves 4: prep: 20 minutes/marinate: 30 minutes/cook: 15–20 minutes

To make the marinade, mix all the ingredients together in a bowl until well combined. Drop the diced chicken thighs into the marinade. Mix well and set aside for 30 minutes.

To cook the chicken, heat the oil to 180°C in a wok or large pan for deep frying. Remove the chicken from the marinade and drain, and place the chicken on kitchen roll to soak up any excess marinade. Deep-fry in batches for 3-4 minutes until golden brown. Transfer to a plate lined with clean kitchen towel and set aside.

Clean the wok or pan and add 2 tablespoons of vegetable oil. Heat to smoking point, then add the chicken followed by the red peppers and onion and stir-fry for 1 minute. Add the garlic and ginger and stir-fry for a further minute. Add both chillies, the spring onions and the Sichuan peppercorn powder. Stir-fry for a further minute then add the sugar, sesame oil and soy sauce. Check the seasoning before serving: this should be hot, spicy, sweet, salty and fragrant from the Sichuan pepper.

Heat another wok on a high heat, add the noodles and soy sauce and mix to coat the noodles evenly with the soy.

In another frying pan heat the pan with the vegetable oil and when smoking hot add the pak choi, cooking for 30 seconds on both sides. Season with a pinch of salt and freshly cracked black pepper.

To serve, put the noodles, pak choi and chicken in a bowl with the fresh coriander leaves and toasted sesame sprinkled on top.

for the marinade
2 tbsps dark soy sauce
1 tbsp rice wine
¼ tsp white pepper powder
3 tsps cornstarch
½ tsp star anise powder
1 small lobe of ginger, finely chopped
2 spring onions, finely chopped
1 teaspoon salt

for the chicken
6 boneless and skinless chicken thighs,
    cut into 2cm dice
1 litre vegetable oil, for frying
1 red pepper, cut into 2cm dice
1 large white onion, cut into
    thin wedges
2 cloves garlic, peeled and finely sliced
1 tbsp peeled ginger, cut into
    fine matchsticks
1 red chilli, finely sliced,
    seeds included
4 dried red chillies, soaked in warm
    water for 15 minutes and cut into
    ½ cm pieces
6 spring onions, cut into 3cm pieces
1 tbsp Sichuan peppercorn powder
1 tsp white sugar
1 tsp sesame oil
1 tbsp light soy sauce
400g egg noodles, pre-soaked
    in cold water
80g light soy sauce
2 tbsps vegetable oil
4 pak choi, cut in half
sea salt & black pepper
4 sprigs fresh coriander, leaves only
1 tsp sesame seeds, toasted

THAI RED CURRY
PORK STIR-FRY

for the curry paste
100ml coconut milk
3 fresh red chillies, seeds removed
1 large shallot, peeled
2 garlic cloves, peeled
1 small lobe of fresh ginger, peeled
1 tbsp fresh lemongrass
½ small bunch coriander
3 dried kaffir lime leaves,
   rehydrated in water
¼ tsp white pepper
¼ tsp ground cumin
¼ tsp ground coriander
2 tbsps paprika

for the curry
2 tbsps vegetable oil
500g Breckland pork leg topside,
   cut into thin strips
300ml coconut milk
1 green pepper, seeds removed
   and sliced
1 red pepper, seeds removed
   and sliced
2 shallots, peeled and finely sliced
75g sliced bamboo shoots,
   drained and rinsed
1 carrot, peeled and cut into
   thin 5cm strips
4 dried kaffir lime leaves,
   rehydrated in water
1 tsp lemon juice
1½ tbsps Thai fish sauce
½ tsp palm sugar
1 green chilli, seeds removed
   and sliced

to serve
200g rice noodles
1 small bunch of fresh Thai basil,
   stalks removed
2 tbsps coriander leaves,
   roughly chopped
1 red chilli, seeds removed
   and sliced

Serves 4 prep: 30 minutes/cook: 15-25 minutes

To make the curry paste, put all the ingredients together in the bowl of a food processor. Blend on a high speed until you have a smooth paste.

To make the curry, put the oil into a large frying pan over a medium to high heat. Add the pork and cook until the meat is slightly coloured. Add the Thai red paste and stir, add the coconut milk and bring to the boil. Turn the heat down to a simmer and add the peppers and shallots. Cook for 1 minute then add the bamboo shoots, carrot, lime leaves, lemon juice, fish sauce, palm sugar and sliced green chillies and stir well together.

To serve, place the rice noodles in a bowl, boil a full kettle of water and pour over the noodles. Leave the noodles for 5 minutes, stirring occasionally. Drain. Just before serving the curry, sprinkle in the Thai basil leaves, coriander and fresh red chillies. Stir gently and remove from the heat. Serve the curry on a bed of rice noodles in a large bowl.

TONKATSU PORK LOIN STEAKS

Serves 4: prep: 20 minutes/marinate: 30 minutes/cook: 30-35 minutes

To make the tonkatsu sauce, mix together all the ingredients.
Use immediately or store in an airtight container in the refrigerator
for up to 1 month.

To make the karashi-style mustard, mix together all the ingredients.
Use immediately or store in an airtight container in the refrigerator for up
to a month.

To make the pork, make very shallow cuts all over pork steaks with the
tip of a knife. Brush lightly on both sides with some of the karashi-style
mustard and leave to marinate for 30 minutes. Coat the pork first with
the seasoned flour, dip into the beaten egg, and then cover with the panko
breadcrumbs. Place in the fridge for 15 minutes to firm up.

Heat a griddle pan on a high heat. Drizzle the spring onions with a little
vegetable oil and when the pan is smoking cook them for 1 minute on each
side until charred.

Heat oil for deep frying to 185°C, and deep-fry the pork in batches until
golden brown and the meat floats on the surface of the oil, about 5-8
minutes, turning once or twice. Drain on kitchen paper.

To serve, cut each steak into 6 pieces. Serve with the tonkatsu sauce,
karashi-style mustard, shredded white cabbage and seared spring onion.

for the tonkatsu sauce
150g tomato ketchup
2 tbsps Worcestershire sauce
2 tbsps dark soy sauce
1 tbsp mirin
1 tsp Dijon mustard
¼ tsp garlic powder

for the karashi-style mustard
6 tsps English mustard powder
6 tsps wasabi paste
4 tsps Dijon mustard
2 tsps Worcestershire sauce
2 tsps light soy sauce
4 tbsps water

for the pork
4 pork loin steaks, fat removed,
*   each around 1cm thick*
200g plain flour, seasoned with
*   salt and white pepper*
1 egg, beaten
50g panko breadcrumbs
1 litre vegetable oil, for frying

for the garnish
8 spring onions, topped and tailed
1 tbsp vegetable oil
1 small white cabbage, finely sliced

WHEN WE DECIDED TO
TURN OUR KNOWLEDGE
INTO A BOOK AND
STARTED TO COMPILE ALL
OUR FAVOURITE FOODS
AND TECHNIQUES, IT
WAS CLEAR WE HAD A
MOUNTAIN OF MATERIAL
FROM ACROSS THE WORLD
TO CHOOSE FROM.

INDEX

Gochujang pork burger with cucumber kimchi, 142

Ham hock and caper terrine, 108

Hampshire rib of pork, 68

Heap's bangers and mash with black kale and crispy shallots, 70

Hog roast belly bites with apple ketchup, 110

Hog roast with apple ketchup, 72

Indian-spiced pulled pork with onion bhajis and mango chutney, 144

Indonesian pork fillet satay with quinoa salad, 146

Louisiana Creole pork steak with dirty rice and lime crème fraiche, 74

Marinated slow-cooked gammon shank with bubble and squeak, 76

Master stock braised Hampshire pork belly, 112

Paprika pork fillet pot, 154

Pork and 'nduja meatballs with spicy tomato sauce, 114

Pork, apple and black pudding sausage roll, 46

Pork fusion taco, 158

Pork ragu bianco, 160

Pulled pork roll with rose harissa and pomegranate molasses, 162

Quiche Lorraine with dry-cured streaky bacon, 48

Rosemary-roasted Hampshire pork loin, 80

Slow-cooked pigs' cheeks in red wine jus, 82

Slow-roasted soy and balsamic glazed Hampshire pork belly
    with sautéed pak-choi, 84

Smoked char siu baby back ribs, 128

Smoked pulled pork carnitas, 126

St Louis Ribs, 130

Teriyaki pork skewers, 118

Thai red curry pork stir-fry, 166

Tonkatsu pork loin steaks, 168

Woodall's Black Combe air-dried ham-wrapped pork fillet with
    Calvados jus, 98

Woodall's British charcuterie platter with Cumberland ring
    and crackling straws, 96

INDEX

CRANSWICK DEVELOPMENT CHEFS
— From left to right: Andy Phillips, Fernando Rampa, Dan Allen, Simon Woods, Mike Flower, Dan McCormack, Steve Mildren, Derek Thorpe, Paul Robinson and Ramadan Zelihic.

CREDITS

Firstly to all the pigs and chickens that have brought this book to life!
We couldn't have done this without you.

Thanks to all the Cranswick chefs that have contributed to the book
– Andy Phillips, Fernando Rampa, Dan Allen, Mike Flower,
Dan McCormack, Steve Mildren, Derek Thorpe, Paul Robinson,
Ramadan Zelihic and Ben Croydon.

Cranswick master butchers Paul Took, Phil Hancox and
Matty O'Loughlin.

Special thanks to Jo Derbyshire at Steelite for arranging the stunning
pieces of crockery used throughout this book.
www.steelite.com

Mia Woods for being Simon's tasting guinea pig throughout the
making of this book – it's a tough job, but someone's got to do it!

Paul Robinson, Yorkshire Gourmet, for the excellent photography.
www.yorkshiregourmet.com

Anthony Hodgson and Amelia Wong for letting a brigade of chefs
and a photographer invade their kitchen and use their amazing garden
for the barbecue shots.

Special thanks to Claire Burcham, Vicky Greenall, Laura Whiting,
Matt Briggs and Andy Napthine for time spent recipe checking and
cooking the recipes at home.

— Jim Brisby

Jim has worked in the food industry at Cranswick since 1995, initially with Martin Heap to develop gourmet sausages and then around the group to develop quality products and upscale the artisan products of Jack Scaife, Woodall's, the Yorkshire Baker, and continental meats.

His knowledge of the food and drink sector resulted in him being appointed to the Cranswick plc board in 2010, and he has been instrumental in developing the strategic direction of the business over the years.

— Simon Woods

Simon started his career at The Savoy Hotel in London before working at some of the best kitchens in the country, including at Wentworth Club, Sopwell House and Luton Hoo.

He took his talents into teaching at Westminster Kingsway College, becoming a qualified lecturer, before moving into a chef development role with Bettys and Taylors of Harrogate. He has won numerous cooking competitions including Gold medals at Hotelympia and the dessert of the year competition in 2010.

Simon is the co-founder of Hog & Beyond, a street food company which uses Cranswick's pork and chicken to showcase local produce with global flavours at food festivals across the country - many of its street food recipes are found in this book.